In Step
with Your
Stepchildren

In Step
with Your
Stepchildren

Building a Strong
One-on-One
Relationship

Karen O'Connor

Beacon Hill Press of Kansas City
Kansas City, Missouri

Copyright 2003
by Karen O'Connor

ISBN 083-412-0453

Printed in the
United States of America

Cover Design: Ted Ferguson

10 9 8 7 6 5 4 3 2 1

For Clifford, Cathleen, Julie, Jim, and Erin

Contents

A Note to the Reader

All the experiences and stories in this book are true. The names, professions, ages, appearances, and other identifying details of some of the people who shared them, however, have been changed to protect their privacy. In those cases, fictional first names or initials are used. Others have granted permission to the author to use their full names, and they are included.

The author thanks all the men and women who contributed to this book.

Introduction

"I DON'T LIKE THE WORD 'STEPPARENT,'" my husband said as I was planning this book. "It sounds so—I don't know—stiff, removed, unfeeling somehow."

I hadn't thought of it that way before, but his comment got me thinking. Stepparents have never been particularly popular. Consider Cinderella's wicked stepmother. She made the poor kid sweep and cook and dress in rags while she pampered and prepared her biological daughters for the king's ball!

We would all probably agree that Cindy's stepmom went too far. She was cruel. But the reality is that we rarely love our "steps" as much as we love our natural or adopted children. We chose *them*.

By contrast, we don't generally choose stepchildren. They come with the man or woman we marry. There's something intangible in a blood relationship that may not exist in the acquired relationship of stepparenting. Some would argue against that statement, but in my informal survey of stepparents, I've found that everyone agreed. People don't line up to be stepparents. Yet millions take on this role every year as the formerly married (those with children) marry again, and the new spouses become stepparents to their new spouse's children. For many it's a "package deal." The husbands and wives don't necessarily think about what's ahead or what will be required of them—or perhaps they don't want to think about it.

I didn't. I was in love. I was ready for a new life. And I was willing (or thought I was) to do whatever it took to have a successful second—and I hoped lasting—marriage.

Did I have a lot to learn! In fact, my discoveries through my own experiences were my motivation for writing this book. Of one thing I'm certain after 19 years of marriage and stepparenting—and that's the absolute importance of building a personal relationship with each stepchild. I'm also certain that we can't come close to achieving this relationship apart from our own relationship with the Spirit of God. We simply can't do it on our own power.

And that ties in with the goal of this book—to encourage you to begin at the beginning, to make sure you're in step with the Holy Spirit (Gal. 5:25) so you're better able to be in step with your stepchildren as individuals worthy of your time, your love, your energy, your respect. Not because you're married to their father or mother and not because they're part of the "package," but because they're a gift from God to you for a particular purpose and season in your life.

Whether your stepchildren are toddlers, teens, in-be-tweens, or adults who are on their own, they have a place in your life. And if you're willing, they'll have a place in your heart as well. Some relationships will come together more easily than others. Some may be difficult and remain that way. Some stepchildren may reject or dismiss your attempts to build a strong one-on-one relationship with them. If so, that's all the more reason to stay in step with the Holy Spirit to guide, guard, and govern your every word and action.

I've found that my stepchildren, unlike my biological children, have challenged my walk as a Christian in a way no one else ever has. I'm humbled by the task but enriched by the opportunity and grateful for the privilege of making a difference for good in their lives when it would have been so much easier to back off and let my husband take full responsibility.

Whether you're a veteran stepparent like me or a brand new one or you're contemplating becoming a stepparent because you're dating or engaged to a man or woman with children, I pray this book will be a source of practical help, wisdom, and inspiration, motivating you to wrap the new children in your life in the quilt of your love and strength—keeping them warm without smothering them!

PART 1
Stepparents Today

1
Happily Ever After

"I'VE ALWAYS WANTED TO BE A MOTHER," Joyce told me excitedly one day as we talked after church. She and her fiancé were in the midst of planning their wedding, and she was looking at ways to include his two children in the ceremony—a 12-year-old boy and an 8-year-old girl. "I adore the kids and they adore me," she added, glowing as she told about the many good times they had shared. "It's as though we're already a family."

Then in a moment of intimacy between us she whispered, "It's practically perfect—except for George's ex-wife. She's consumed with jealousy and is determined to make things miserable for us." Her bubbly demeanor suddenly turned serious, and I could see a touch of hostility creep into her eyes. "I don't know why she can't leave us alone."

After a few more moments of conversation, I hugged her, assuring her of my prayers for wisdom, and hurried off, my heart pounding because of the memories the conversation brought to the surface. I remember having similar thoughts about my ex-husband's new wife—my children's new stepmother. And I had my biased viewpoint about my stepchildren's mother—someone I had never even met! I was incredibly naive about the role of stepparent and the impact it would have on my life and the children.

My White Knight

Charles was the father of two teenagers, and I was the mother of three when we met. After we married, he was suddenly the stepfather of my three, and I became the stepmother of his two. Some friends wished us luck. Others said they would pray for us. Still others looked at me as if to say, "Do you know what you're getting into?"

I thought I did. Charles and I loved each other, we loved our kids, and we made a vow to uphold one another through sickness and health, poverty and wealth—and through the teenaged years and beyond of our collective five. He was the man I had hoped for, the knight who would rescue me and carry me off to a new city, a new dream, a brand-new life.

Stepparenting was the last thing on my mind. I was focused on "my man" and myself. Even if I had thought about it, I doubt that I would have been concerned. Charles's daughter, Cathy, lived with her mother 2,000 miles away, and his son, Cliff, had just started college and moved into his first apartment with a roommate. I had very little contact with either of my stepchildren on a day-to-day basis.

Help Wanted!

I was fond of Charles's children, and they were sweet and polite toward me. Charles thought my kids were great. They laughed at his jokes and enjoyed the special attention they received from him whenever we were together. I was sure we would all live happily ever after!

But real life, even in the best of families, is not a fairy tale. I came down to earth with a thud. Charles and my oldest daughter were suddenly at odds. My stepdaughter, who had been a pal during the summer her dad and I dated, now seemed distant when she visited, flinging accusatory looks at me one minute and feigning affection the next.

Soon I began to wonder if I had made the worst mistake of my life. Parenting teens without a partner was difficult enough, but now it seemed that parenting *with* a partner and adding stepchildren to the mix was even worse. There were so many personalities to deal with—so many needs and wants to meet. I felt inadequate, unappreciated, and mostly overwhelmed.

I had started to believe that we were the only couple on the planet who didn't know how to lead our children and stepchildren or how to meet them where they were. I wondered if it was because the kids were constantly coming and going between two households rather than living with us on a permanent basis.

Charles and I had one another consistently. Who did they have? Half a parent, maybe? They hadn't had to share us with anyone while we were single, but now that there were new spouses, they may have wondered where they fit into our lives and in the new family arrangement.

They never asked in so many words where they fit, but they expressed their concern in other ways. Their communication took some interesting forms: grunts, grumbling, angry looks, slammed doors. Answers were short, feelings suppressed, hostility apparent.

In hope and frustration, we reached out to our church prayer team and to other stepparents. We needed prayer and support, certainly—but we also needed advice.

We received helpful and encouraging insights. The stepparents we spoke with admitted that we had some unique challenges because none of our children lived with us full time. However, we also learned that circumstances aren't the only factor to consider. Kids, like adults, have individual personalities, and there were bound to be hurts and misunderstandings when we bumped into one another—by accident or even on purpose! We were reminded to take it easy, not to overwhelm or overindulge them in an effort to gain favor, to be ourselves, and to trust God to lead us. In short, no blueprint was available! We needed to proceed with respect for ourselves and for each child—different as we were from one another.

DIFFERENCES MAKE A DIFFERENCE

My stepdaughter, Cathy, is a peacemaker by nature. When she feels stressed, however, she withdraws. And she doesn't like anyone to prod her when she doesn't want to talk.

My stepson, Cliff, is congenial and pleasant to be around. He has a sense of humor and is open to working things out. Since he was about to enter college when I met his dad, he never lived with us after we were married. (Maybe that's why I thought of him as the easiest of the five.)

My daughters, Erin and Julie, were the most verbal of the bunch, and they had plenty to say—good and bad—to my husband when they were with us. Their sometimes harsh and direct comments in the early months were hard on him, because he likes everyone to get along, and they hadn't voiced their opinions so strongly before we were married.

My son, Jim, who was trying to work through his anger about his dad's and my divorce, decided to keep his distance the first few years. He didn't want anyone parenting him!

So much for fairy tale dreams and happily-ever-after endings. They don't always exist, and we can't create them. Life is hard. Stepparenting makes life harder still. But it also presents opportunities for growth and grace that are unique and worthy of our commitment of time and energy. As I look back, I wouldn't change a thing.

The difficult years are behind us now. Our children are grown. Three of the five are married and have families of their own. We've come through the storms of those early years, and I can say with certainty that we wouldn't be where we are today without the Holy Spirit—guiding, guarding, and governing our every going-out and coming-in. It wasn't easy—but it was valuable.

We are a family—not just a blended family, but an extended family—that includes ex-spouses and their new partners, step-siblings and now their spouses and children, grandparents and step-grandparents, and a host of aunts, uncles, and cousins. I can't think of an event when we've all been together at the same time, but we're always—to my way of thinking—together in spirit. Whether consciously or not, each member has contributed to the life I live today. I've learned from the good and the bad and the horrible, and I thank God for seeing me through all of it.

STEPPARENTS' CLUB: SIGN UP HERE

Maybe you can relate to some of my experiences. Or perhaps you've traveled a very different path. Whatever your story, we do have something in common—stepchildren and the role of stepparent. We're all part of a big group. I call it the Stepparents' Club, and membership offers the same rights and privileges to everyone who joins. We don't have monthly meetings, there are no financial dues, and no one will call and ask you to chair a committee. But still we're together in mind and heart and spirit as we discover the many benefits and opportunities that are ours as members of a universal association.

As I look at my friends who are stepparents, I see that there's no one way to be or to behave. In fact, there seems to be a freedom today that stepparents of years past might not have experienced or dared express. Hurray! We get to have a life, as the saying goes, and still be considered upstanding members of the Stepparents' Club. One doesn't exclude the other.

My husband and I, as well as many of our friends, have discovered how to be good, caring stepparents without guilt and without pressure from outside expectations. We can be who we are right now. Stereotypes are out; authenticity is in. You can be who you are and still be a terrific stepparent whether you're raising your stepkids, hosting them on weekends, or visiting them in another city.

The important things haven't changed, namely the presence of a stepparent in the life of a child and your presence in the life of your stepchildren.

Who We Are

With freedom, however, comes responsibility. Being a stepparent involves a lot more than who we're married to, how often we interact with our stepchildren, or how we express our individuality. More important is who we are in our relationships with the children themselves. Our stepchildren are not impressed that we're married to their father or mother (some are openly hostile, in fact) or awed by our professional credentials or excited about our passion for golfing or gardening. They *are* interested in seeing how we relate to *them*, if we're authentic with *them*, if we care about *them*, if we want the best for *them* in this new family situation.

Following are some of the behaviors stepchildren value in us as stepmothers and stepfathers.

We Depend on God's Grace

My grace is sufficient for you, for my power is made perfect in weakness (2 Cor. 12:9).

"Janet, will you pray for me? I'm trying to get ready for an exam, and I'm terrified."

Following those words on the phone from her stepdaughter Lynn, my friend Janet began praying immediately. Later Janet told me that experience was the breakthrough she had hoped for in her relationship with Lynn.

Janet had married Lynn's dad a year after Lynn's mother had died, and Lynn was still holding a grudge three years later at age 15. "No matter what I did, she kept her distance," said Janet. "I knew she needed a mother's love, but she seemed determined not to accept it from me."

Janet had invited Lynn to play tennis, to shop, to go to a tea at church. She offered to listen to Lynn's complaints or problems, but Lynn turned down all invitations.

"Imagine how surprised I was when she called for prayer, of all things," said Janet.

I wasn't totally surprised, because I know my friend, and I believed it was just a matter of time before Lynn reached out to Janet—a person of much depth with a genuinely caring heart. Here is a woman who depends on God's grace, and she certainly needed an extra measure of it in her marriage (her first) to Lynn's father. Lynn and her dad had been inseparable since Lynn's mother's death, so it was understandable that Lynn would see Janet as an intruder.

But God is faithful, and He sows the seeds of reconciliation—often behind the scenes. Then, at just the right time, the fruit is ripe for the picking. But if Janet had not been ready, she might have missed the opportunity for this precious connection.

We Express Love

Dear children, let us not love with words or tongue but with actions and in truth (1 John 3:18).

"I never thought that having stepchildren could teach me how to love another woman's children as much as my own," said Pat Evans.

But it did. The lesson came through dealing with the children's birth mother. "So many times I've literally had to bite my lip so I wouldn't say something that would affect the kids' relationship with her."

Pat remembers making sure the children had dinner *before* their mother picked them up from their visits. "If I didn't, they usually wouldn't eat," she said.

Pat also recalls how she worried about her stepdaughter when she wasn't with Pat and her husband. "I told her often that she could count on me to pick her up anywhere for any reason if she got into trouble or had a problem. I made sure she had my phone number." Sometimes she also worried that the girl's mother would have Pat arrested for kidnapping or worse.

"But when I put all this into the Lord's hands, I felt peaceful," said Pat. "Two months after asking God for His will for us and the children, the kids moved in with us and remained in our home until they were adults."

At times Pat had to remind herself that she had prayed for a husband. "God just blessed me a little more than I expected!" she added.

We Value Relationships

Sons are a heritage from the LORD, children a reward from him (Ps. 127:3).

Stepparents are generally people who care! If they didn't, they wouldn't take on relationships that include other people's children. Why should they? No one needs more stress, more responsibility, more challenges. I believe those who consciously become stepparents are men and women who want to make a difference in children's lives.

Josh is a good example.

"You ought to close the door on Matt and never look back—especially since he's not even your own. He doesn't deserve a stepdad as fine as you." When Josh heard those words from someone he counted as a friend, he cringed. He knew the man meant well. But how could he give up on 16-year-old Matt—his stepson, his wife's firstborn, the boy he had held, rocked, and fished with?

Josh had noticed Matt withdrawing over the previous months, but he chalked it up to adolescence. His wife wasn't concerned. She said he was detaching, growing up, and that they just needed to be patient.

"Then his mother found out he had been skipping class and drinking," said Josh. "It was one of our darkest times. But I wasn't going to let go of Matt that easily. He's in a treatment program now. We might have a long road ahead, but I care about that boy, and I'm going to stick by him."

We Forgive Readily

Forgive, and you will be forgiven (Luke 6:37).

Most of us can forgive quickly the careless movement of a child that results in a spill or a broken dish or a smudge of dirt from muddy sneakers. But what about the deep wounds that result from broken commitments, hurtful words calculated to inflict pain, or neglect and indifference on the part of older stepchildren?

We can easily be tempted to nurse our grudges, blame our spouses when our stepchildren hurt and disappoint us, and make the family pay for every little grievance we endure. At times like these, we must look to the Holy Spirit—the Spirit of Jesus, the Paraclete ("the one who comes alongside"), who carried to the Cross the entire burden of our sin and pain. As He forgave even the people who treated Him cruelly, He modeled the forgiveness we can extend to our stepchildren.

Ellen Bergh knows about the challenge of forgiveness firsthand. "It has been one of the most painful experiences of my life," she said, "to watch my teenaged stepdaughter hurt and reject her father, then come back into his life when she was in her mid-30s and married with children."

Ellen said they "welcomed Kim with open arms. Our natural daughter was thrilled to meet her half-sister for the first time." But nothing good came of it. Kim continued to play her game of trying to estrange family members from one another and ultimately rejected them.

The relationship has not cleared up. But Ellen said she believes the Holy Spirit has shown them how to sow love, even though it's difficult, and how to forgive and let go. "We continue to pray for her and for her children."

What do Ellen and her husband do with their pain and the love and energy they would like to pour into that family? "We look for ways to be of service in other parts of our lives," said Ellen. And they trust God to do what they clearly cannot do on their own.

We Laugh Easily

Our mouths were filled with laughter, our tongues with songs of joy (Ps. 126:2).

Stepparents who forgive readily usually laugh easily. Perhaps more importantly, they can laugh at themselves. They're not afraid to admit their own weaknesses and poke a little fun at themselves. They enjoy the small things—a funny joke, a silly game, a bit of teasing, the playful antics of a young child, the offbeat humor of a teenager. They see the light instead of the darkness.

Pat Evans said they included laughter and relaxation in their family life through their tradition of going to Mammoth Lakes, California, every winter to ski and just be together.

"The boys went in the truck, and the girls went in the van, and we connected by CB radio—this was before cell phones," explained Pat. "My daughter and stepdaughter who are 18 months apart in age talked nonstop for six hours! We all still talk about our road trips and how much we learned and laughed and cried and planned for the future. I taught them how to set goals, how to cook and sew—yes, even in the van—but most important, how to pray and to rely on God for everything."

We Admit Our Limitations

But when he, the Spirit of truth, comes, he will guide you into all truth (John 16:13).

One of the great blessings of the 12-step programs is the opportunity they present to look at our weaknesses and limitations, assess our strengths, and make whatever changes are possible in order to achieve the serenity we all desire.

Step Four directs people in the program to carry out a "searching and fearless moral inventory" of themselves. This means we're to look with determination and commitment—to *search*—not merely glance around and then duck out before we find something we need to handle. And we're to conduct our search without fear. If fear is present, we certainly can feel and acknowledge it, but we must continue to search anyway.

This has not been an easy task for me or for anyone I know, but it has been one of the most fruitful. I not only uncovered my limitations and character defects but also discovered many strengths and abilities that had been under wraps because of my previous reluctance to start the process.

Once I entered into it, however, I felt light and free—similar to the good feeling that comes when you dig into a closet bulging with things you should have tossed out years ago. My limitations were nothing to be ashamed of, and I began to see myself as quite normal. I came down from my ivory tower of self-righteousness and joined the human race. I discovered that it was all right to say, "I need help," "I don't know," "That's too much to ask," or "I can't do that right now."

Today it's OK for me to set limits. Some find that harder than others. We want to be liked! And some of us may think that if we say "no" or "not now" we might slip down a notch or two on the popularity poll. And it's true—we might. But so what? I believe our stepchildren will respect us for it. By modeling our humanness, we will be giving them permission to do the same. And when we lean on God, He shows us by His Spirit what is true, and we can relax. There is no need to try to be someone we are not.

Some stepparents (and I'm one of them) don't like mass confusion, clutter, or wild play and high-volume noise. Some stepparents also don't pick up the kids' dirty laundry. An occasional shoe or book, maybe, but smelly clothes—never! Bedtimes are enforced, and everyone pitches in with dishes after a meal.

Others prefer to keep a casual home. The door's always open to friends and neighbors. Last-minute dinner guests are welcome. Maybe these stepparents don't mind noise or rough play and are not opposed to unplanned sleepovers or baking a batch of cookies at 10:00 p.m.

You probably have limits of your own, both physical and emotional. Or maybe your personality type is more passive than passionate or more controlling than carefree. Such differences impose limitations. Whatever the reason, I believe it's important for us to know ourselves in this way so we can be fully present to our stepchildren within the boundaries of our temperament and preferences.

We can't be everything they want—or even everything we want to be. We are who we are—and it's OK as long as we speak and act truthfully.

We Try New Experiences

The Lord will open . . . the storehouse of his bounty (Deut. 28:12).

"I never thought I'd sleep in a tent," said Maureen. "I like my own mattress under me and my favorite comforter over me!" Yet Maureen didn't pass up the opportunity to join her stepdaughter for a mother-daughter youth group campout. She admits that it isn't something she wants to do again anytime soon, but she's glad she went and she is grateful for the closeness she felt with her stepdaughter.

Other stepparents have confided that many new experiences have opened up to them through their stepchildren.

- hot air ballooning
- picking apples and turning them into a pie
- rollerblading
- finger painting
- teaching Sunday School
- reading mysteries
- ice skating

We See the Big Picture

There is a time for everything, and a season for every activity under heaven (Eccl. 3:1).

I remember the first time I saw the big picture. I was hiking with some friends on a trail that seemed to be an endless row of ups and downs. We would gain 200 feet and then lose them, gain and lose, gain and lose. It seemed we would never make it to the top of the mountain.

I was almost ready to turn back when a hiker who had gone on ahead of me shouted down the hill, "Come on up. The panorama is awesome!" That's all I needed to hear. I raced on, and soon I was viewing the big picture. Finally I could see that despite the highs and lows along the way, overall we were heading up!

Stepparents often have the experience and the distance to see the big picture in a way that natural parents may miss because of their emotional involvement with their children. We can bring clarity out of confusion and peace to panicky situations. We know the tough times come and go, but overall, the family is going up.

We can comfort our mates and stepchildren in times of crisis, help them gain perspective on a problem by sharing our own experiences, lend a hand in a moment of need, and most important, remind ourselves and them to turn to the Holy Spirit for guidance, with gratitude for what a situation can teach us about ourselves.

"It took me a long time to thank God for the difficulties," said Mary Jane. "I now know that I learned so much from these experiences. For example, I remember once when our middle son, Trevor, was having problems at school. Our minister encouraged him to start lifting weights as a way to work out his anger. He told Trevor that this discipline is similar to going to church. Sometimes it's hard to do, but it's good for you."

We could look at stepparenting in the same way. It is hard—but it's also good for us in that we're stretched in body, mind, and spirit. Sometimes we're so tired at night that we just fall into bed, our bodies aching for rest. Our minds are restless with the problems of the day, and our spirits are sagging.

Mary Jane recalls when her stepsons, ages 9 and 10, came to live with her and her husband. "I realized I was no longer just a wife," said Mary Jane. "I was now a stepparent, and I took my job seriously."

But she soon felt challenged in ways she hadn't imagined. The boys were aggressive, rude, and they swore—totally the opposite of what she and their father wanted or expected from disciplined children.

They called her "Mom" but treated her as if she were a servant. Their biological mother, on the other hand, played bridge most days and evenings and never provided a positive environment for the boys when she had them.

Mary Jane recalled how her mother-in-law came to her rescue by praying with her. "My relationship with the Lord provided the spiritual food I needed to survive," she added.

"I learned I couldn't control everything, even though I tried," Mary Jane said. "My degree is in child development, so I was determined to get to the bottom of my stepchildren's problems and fix them. Then they would love our family life like no other." But it didn't work out that way. Mary Jane admitted her expectations were unrealistic.

She decided to take training to become a facilitator for a "Love and Logic Discipline" parenting program at a local hospital. She then taught classes twice a year. "This experience challenged me," she said. "My life had been so organized and under control until I became a stepparent. Then suddenly everything was out of control.

"I knew I needed God," she added. "I started trusting Him instead of myself. And my prayer life changed for the better."

STEPPARENT HAVEN

When someone asked my husband what he liked best about being a stepparent, he paused and then answered confidently, "I've been able to contribute to three individuals in a way that changed their lives and mine," he said. "I remember one of my stepdaughters telling me that I had been a father to her in a way that she needed. Wow! That blew me away. I don't think I worked at making that happen. But the fact that it did occur was an enormous blessing to me—and apparently to her too."

You probably have your own response to that question. And like us, you probably have a ready answer when asked what you like least about stepparenting. But I don't want to draw attention to that. The challenges are always there. I want to focus on what works, what produces good, what deepens and broadens our experiences as stepparents. And I believe that walking in step with the Spirit of God is at the heart of being able to walk in step with our stepchildren.

He is our haven, our shelter, our high tower, and when things get tough, He's the one to run to for encouragement and the grace to start again.

Building a Strong One-on-One Relationship

1. List your stepchildren by name and age. Jot down two things about each one that makes him or her special to you. Then write at least two ways you can interact with each in a personal way. (Examples: water-play with a toddler; ride bikes with an elementary-school child; skateboard with a middle schooler; invite a teenager out to dinner, a play, concert, or professional sporting event, and so on.) Next, do it!

2. Volunteer at your stepchild's school or participate in one of his or her hobbies or after-school activities such as Scouts or Little League.

3. Write a personal letter to your stepchild—whatever his or her age—for a birthday or other special occasion.

2
Lives of Our Own

BETTY LOOKED AT ME FROM ACROSS THE TABLE as we sipped tea at the hotel café where we had stopped for lunch. She thumbed through the photos of my children and stepchildren.

"I think I'm jealous," she said playfully. "You seem to like Cliff and Cathy. I can't say the same for my stepkids. I wanted to love them as if they were my own, but so far I don't. I'm not even sure I *like* them very much. Isn't that awful?"

Betty had remarried in her late 40s. Her husband was a widower with two teenagers at the time they met. She was excited about the prospect of being part of a family after having lived alone for so long. But the children weren't eager for their dad to remarry, and they didn't appreciate Betty's attempts at being their mom. She was beginning to feel that she had made a huge mistake.

I understood. I remember my desire to win over Cathy when she came to live with us as a young adult. Suddenly our relationship was very different from the one we had had while she was a teen who visited during the summer. She seemed to resent my being there—even though it was my home. I realized some months later that I was trying too hard. Instead of letting things unfold, I was attempting to make something happen between us. I was very much out of step with the Holy Spirit and certainly out of step with Cathy.

One day I got fed up working so hard at something I wasn't even sure I wanted! So I gave it up and turned my attention and my energy to my own life. I talked to her, of course, and made myself available if she had a need. But basically I got on with my routine—aerobics in the morning, writing in the afternoon, meeting friends, spending time with my husband. In a matter of weeks, things changed again—for the better. Cathy bought me a gift for Mother's Day, came into my home office to chat in the evenings, and was warmer and friendlier than she had ever been.

I learned a lot from that experience: I can't make anyone love me—or even like me. I'm responsible to the Lord for the life He gave me. And I'm to live it out under His grace regardless of what's going on with the people around me— including my stepchildren. It was clear that as soon as I took back my own life, I was a happier, more authentic person to be around, and everything began to improve.

Root Causes

If you struggle with your role as stepparent, giving away too much of yourself because of your need to be needed or backing off for fear of being consumed by your stepchildren, you're not free to be yourself either as a stepparent or as a person. It may be time to look at the possible roots of your beliefs and behavior.

Maybe you can relate to some of the following causes, which were compiled from comments shared by a variety of stepparents. Like them, you may find that your feelings of inadequacy, guilt, or resistance stem from your own childhood.

You grew up in an emotionally distant family. You did not see honest and open displays of affection, approval, or acceptance. Nor did you see anyone model true grief, anger, or sadness. As you grew up in this climate, you probably soon discovered that the people around you couldn't handle your strong emotions either. If you did express yourself honestly, you were told to "cool it" or to "be more considerate of others." You began to believe that you didn't count. What others wanted from you became more important than what you wanted for yourself.

A child who comes from such an environment is very likely to live his or her entire life trying to be someone other than who he or she really is. And that behavior will carry over to our stepparenting experiences, because the older we get, the more our fears intensify if we're not aware of them. We abandon ourselves further as we cling more and more to our families, seeking identity and refuge in our spouses and stepchildren. Or our response may be to push them away or hang back because we can't handle the intimacy involved.

Caron Loveless traces some of her stepparenting challenges to the relationship she had with her stepmother, who was harsh, unloving, extremely strict, and unaffectionate.

"She brought a sizable amount of emotional baggage into her marriage to my father," said Caron, "a marriage that was going south by the time my father contracted cancer seven years later."

Before Caron's dad died, his wife legally adopted his children. She later remarried, and then Caron and her siblings had two stepparents—neither of whom cared for them as they deserved.

You learned to control others by expressing your dependence on them. You may have been taught that the only way to hold onto others—and thus your own life—was to be dependent on those close to you: first parents, then your spouse, and finally your children if you have them, and stepchildren. At this point in your life, you might welcome time to yourself, some quiet and peace, a hobby or part-time job that would be just for you, but you feel poorly equipped to do any of these things because you're not convinced you can or should.

Children who grow up depending on others for their happiness and fulfillment are never authentically happy or fulfilled. No one can do that for you. Your relationship with your spouse and stepchildren then will not be genuine;

rather, it will be a dependency that stems from the lack in your own childhood. And you'll feel resentful when these people don't appreciate all you do for them.

This can be especially true for stepparents who often try hard to build close relationships with their stepchildren. They may even invest too much of themselves in an effort to make up for the lack they felt in their lives as children.

You accepted the message that you weren't important enough to develop your full potential as a person. I think this is a chronic state for many people in our culture. They don't know who they are. And this is true not only of non-Christians. Many believers live out their lives under the same dark cloud. They don't know who they are in Christ, and they don't know their places in the world. They have not been encouraged or taught to believe that they're valuable just because of who they are. So they "create" value by performing or doing things for others.

If they become stepparents, they try too hard—putting their attention and energy into this new role and depending on it to fulfill them. Some admit they've looked forward to rescuing their stepchildren from their "evil" birth parents! Such men and women need permission to explore their own identities and discover aspects of life that are not dependent on what other people—especially their spouses or stepchildren—think of them.

You feel worthy only when you spend time, energy, and money on your spouse or stepchildren. If you grew up in a home where your mother was a full-time caregiver, then your sense of worth may depend on how much you do for your family and others and how little you do for yourself. Even if you work outside the home, you may feel compelled to use your earnings to support your stepchildren's lifestyle or to pay for all of their school tuition or clothing needs instead of acknowledging that this is a shared responsibility with the children's birth parents.

You provide the birthday parties for your stepson or stepdaughter, the music lessons, or the summer camp fees, even if it means going without something necessary in your own life.

Or you may take pride in being the "loving" or "caring" parent. Devoting yourself to your stepfamily in this way makes you feel good about yourself. You may even notice that you *have* to do it—but then you realize you feel resentful when there's too little time and energy left for yourself.

You live in a state of longing. Stepparents who live through others are a burden not only to those persons but to themselves as well, because no other individual can fulfill them. They find themselves living in a constant state of desire, never quite sure what it is they want or need but feeling irritable and discontent.

Perhaps as a child you were continually denied even your most basic desires. If you asked for a bicycle like those other kids had, you were told there was no money for that. If you wanted to purchase a special book or attend an event or participate in a sport, you may have been ridiculed or dismissed for whatever reason.

So you grew up with a deep hunger that was never satisfied. As an adult, you may still experience these emotions, especially if you're a parent and a stepparent where doing double duty is the norm. Instead of one soccer or baseball game, you have to attend two. You find yourself constantly yielding or adjusting to someone else's schedule in order to coordinate with the schedule of another set of parents and grandparents.

If you recognize these feelings, it may be time to open up to your needs and wants and to give yourself some of the pleasures you were denied as a child.

"Being a stepmother of two grown stepchildren who are nine and eleven years younger than me," said Sandy Peckham, "forced me to face some core issues in my life that I had not faced until that time. They say that parents often reflect upon their own lives at whatever stage their children are experiencing. I noticed early in the relationship with my stepchildren that I had some unfinished business in my own life regarding my young adult years."

Sandy realized she had some lessons to learn, and being a stepparent is the route God used to teach her. "I had to give up self-pity," she said. "Because I married for the first time in my mid-30s, I struggled as my stepchildren found spouses while they were in their twenties. That's what I had wanted for my life. While I was still a new bride myself, I became the stepmother of the bride!"

Sandy had to face her broken dream of not finding a mate when she was younger. "I blamed God for it," she said, "and concluded that He must love me less than He loved everyone else whom He blessed with husbands while they were 20-something."

Sandy had held on to this dream and others since she was a little girl. "As time marched on and that dream didn't come true," said Sandy, "I hid the hurt and disappointment from myself until I saw my stepchildren marry."

The Lord led Sandy through several more issues until she learned the truth of Isa. 55:8-9: *"My thoughts are not your thoughts, neither are your ways my ways," declares the LORD. "As the heavens are higher than the earth, so are my ways higher than your ways and my thoughts than your thoughts."*

"The biggest lesson I learned during that time," Sandy said, "was that God has a purpose for each person who calls Him Father, and we can't look to our circumstances to determine how much He loves us! To this day, I'm so grateful to the Lord for His patience with me as I learned this lesson."

Six years later, Sandy is getting a better understanding of how God is working in her life and in the lives of her stepchildren. "Today we're all using our individual gifts for the advancement of God's kingdom," she said.

Men and women who seek fulfillment for themselves find they enjoy their spouses and stepchildren more than those who pour all their energy into the family without any thought for themselves. They no longer make the family their only focus but instead include them as part of a larger life.

They also notice their families are more interested in them when they bring something new and stimulating to the relationships, such as an interest in painting, history, or science.

You feel that life is passing you by. I've heard it said there are four kinds of people in the world: those who organize the parade, those who march in it, those who stand on the sidewalk and watch it, and those who ask, "What parade?"

Where do you fit? If you're one who's lingering on the sidewalk as others step out and pass you, you may feel angry. You may even feel competitive with your stepchildren as they move into the world and claim their spots, going to school, playing sports, discovering new interests, experiencing the arts. Maybe you were denied these opportunities when you were growing up, and now, watching them, you're reminded of how shallow your life has become.

But it's never too late to join the parade. In fact, many stepparents claim it's their stepchildren who have inspired them to march! There are now groups and clubs in churches and communities throughout the country specifically geared to adults who want to learn new skills, take up a hobby, or volunteer their time and talent. No one needs to stand on the sidewalk—unless he or she chooses to.

Ps. 37:23 reminds us that "If the LORD delights in a man's way, he makes his steps firm." So march on, knowing that God will lead the way.

BUILDING A STRONG ONE-ON-ONE RELATIONSHIP

1. Consider the root causes of your resistance to intimacy or guilt regarding the amount of time you spend or don't spend with your stepchildren or your tendency to overfocus on them. Do you relate to any of the root causes listed in this chapter? Would you like to change your behavior? If so, in what way?

2. What have you been putting off that you would like to experience? What steps could you take to make this a reality?

3. How do you think nurturing yourself could also nurture your stepchildren and your spouse? Give specific examples.

3
More than a Friend—Less than a Natural Parent

"THIS STEPPARENTING THING is pretty tricky," Paul said following a Sunday morning church service. He came up front for prayer, and I was part of the prayer team that day. "I'm not exactly a parent since my stepchildren don't live with me full-time," he explained. "I've only been in their lives for two years, but I'm more than a friend."

Paul said he needed prayer for discernment and wisdom as his stepson and stepdaughter entered adolescence. "I have a stake in their lives," he said, "and I want to be an example they can be proud of."

I was touched by his humility. First we talked about how stepparenting offers a special opportunity to be both a parent and a friend—a unique relationship that stepparents can create since their status is voluntary. They do not have to fit a mold—but rather be a person from whom their stepchildren can learn and be inspired through interaction, observation, and example.

IN SPIRIT AND IN TRUTH

Some stepparents dive right into the relationship and don't hold back. Lena is such a person. She married a man with one daughter, Heather, aged 10. Lena remembered her own growing-up years as an only child, and she didn't want to make the same mistake with Heather that her stepmother had made with her.

Lena's parents divorced when she was seven, and her father then married a woman who had little time for or interest in Lena. She went through the motions during the girl's weekend visits with her dad, such as going out with her dad and her for lunch or spending the day with them at the zoo, but Lena noticed how the woman clung to her dad and seemed to watch the clock until it was time to return Lena to her mother.

She grew up feeling tolerated instead of loved and cherished as she went from one home to the other, never sure of where she belonged. Today Lena is determined to create a different experience for her stepdaughter, Heather.

"I've come to love Heather as my own," said Lena. "It's taken time to win her trust, to show her I care. First I had to realize that I matter in her life. I'm the adult, and it's up to me to create a relationship with her."

As I listened to Lena talk about her experience, it occurred to me there must be thousands, if not millions, of stepparents across North America who overlook opportunities of their own to reach out to their stepchildren, to influence and inspire them with companionship, conversation, simple caring gestures that say, "You're special. You're important. You matter to me—apart from my relationship with your mother or father."

Some stepparents may hold back because they feel like a third or fourth wheel. The child already has a mom and dad. "What can I add?" they may ask. Because they don't recognize their importance as individuals, they don't see their relevance to their stepchildren. So instead of giving what only they can give, they hang back, willing to live on the periphery of their stepchildren's lives instead of being part of the center.

Others stay on the sidewalk because they don't know how or where to enter the child's life, or they're not sure it would make any difference if they did. They don't realize that who they are matters and that who they are makes a difference. Who you are is a gift in more ways than you might imagine. You won't find out until you take the risk of stepping up and speaking out.

Now is the time to begin participating in more active and meaningful ways. If you're already doing that, then you know what it is to pass on wisdom, knowledge, and experience so that your stepchildren's lives will be enriched and deepened.

If you're not involved in a personal way and you want to be, spend some time looking into your life and the lives of your stepchildren. Ask the Holy Spirit to quicken your heart and open your eyes to ways you can build a bridge between you. What could you share about yourself that would help them know you on a deeper level? What would you like to know about them? How could you contribute in a way that will draw them out and help them grow as individuals?

Here are some things to consider:

Be a Playmate

Young children are thrilled when you sit on the floor with them and play a game. They don't like spectators in their lives. They love participants. How about checkers, Monopoly, CandyLand, Parcheesi, Clue, or dominoes? Playing opens a way to be together without stress.

If they want to ride bikes or roller-blade, get out there with them. Let the Spirit lead you. I've ice-skated, climbed trees, and hiked through a cave in the desert.

Young kids love to play tag in a swimming pool, build a fort with blankets and boxes, and stage a race at the park or in the backyard. You might be surprised at how close you'll feel toward one another when you spend time laughing and simply playing.

Maybe you're not the type to roughhouse or chase or roll in the sand. So be it. What *do* you enjoy? You can engage children in making crafts, cooking meals, playacting, reading a story. The important thing is being together in a light-hearted way that shows them you care.

It's all in the way you present it.

"I'm not up for tag, but how about coloring or playing with clay?"

"I need some fresh air. How about a game of catch or a walk to the park?"

Mostly, our younger stepchildren just want to be with us. They love attention and togetherness. They're usually willing to compromise if we are.

Be a Pal

Stepchildren often think of their stepparents as pals—in a different way than they think of their own parents. If you're a fun person to be with, they'll want to spend time with you whether you're going fishing or swimming, running errands, watching football, working on a puzzle, or baking a cake.

One stepdad told me that he has some of his best talks with his stepson when he takes him along to the hardware store, computer store, or bookstore. "It's easier to talk somehow, especially when we're sharing a common interest—like sports or computers."

A stepmom can be a pal to boys as well as to girls. Find out what the kids are excited about. Learn something about that interest and then plan an event around it. For example, Robbie said she took her stepson to a snake exhibit at a local museum and was surprised to find how much she enjoyed it. She came home with a real understanding of why Jay wanted a snake for a pet and was then willing to let him have one.

"I cringed at the idea at first," she said, "but when I prayed for guidance about how to handle this sticky situation, I felt led to learn about his interest instead of making a decision that worked just for me. Now we have this thing between us about snakes. It's quite funny when I think of it, but it's brought us closer than ever before."

Be a Friend

Children value friendships. It's important to them to have friends at school, to be considered a friend by one of their peers, and to know that you're not just the person who married their mom or dad but one who is a friend to them in their own right.

The *Thorndike Barnhart Dictionary* defines the word *friend* as "a person who knows and likes another; a chum, crony, companion; a person who favors and supports."

As a friend to your stepchildren, you're one who "knows and likes" them. And as your friend, they can get to know and like you if you encourage them to do so. Notice that the definition does not qualify. The phrase "knows and likes" is inclusive of all parts of the individual—both the strengths and weaknesses. We all need this kind of "favor and support," regardless of our age.

Children, still learning and growing and feeling their way in life, need someone to stand by them and affirm and forgive them as well as keep them accountable when they push the limit. They are by nature more sensitive than many adults, so they appreciate stepparents who go out of their way to offer a hand of friendship—at any age.

Donna Wyland said that being a stepmother has "required me to look further beyond myself than I ever thought possible in order to fit unrelated people into my heart."

She talked about a time when her stepson, Christopher, her husband's youngest son, asked to live with her and his dad to see what it was like compared to living with his mother and brothers.

"We agreed he could live with us from September through December of that year," she said, "but I never realized what I had gotten myself into until he moved in.

"He was completely delightful, but I was torn to pieces each day wondering how I could keep him occupied and happy during the time he was with us. I found myself making snowmen after school when homework was done and trying to come up with some kind of inventive and exciting dinner to cook each night that would make him want to stay."

But Donna learned an amazing truth about Christopher and about most kids one night after her daughter had gone to bed. "This young boy who had watched me interact naturally with my daughter as I played games with her and read to her each night approached me as I sat in front of the television set. He looked at me with eyes wide open. 'Donna,' he said, 'would you mind if I sat in your lap for a while too?' It nearly brought tears to my eyes. This gangly young boy needed me just as much as my own daughter did. Stepparenting wasn't about keeping him busy and happy. It was about loving him—and being a friend."

Be a Spiritual Model

As Christians, we have a unique opportunity to share our faith with our stepchildren, to demonstrate our love for Jesus, and to help them build their own relationships with the Holy Spirit. How inspiring it is for a child to see a stepparent as a spiritual model! You can enrich your stepchildren's faith walk by reading to them, listening to worship music, and participating together in youth events. A woman I spoke with said one of her best childhood memories was of her stepdad reading Bible stories to her before she went to sleep at night.

You might also volunteer to help at the youth club at the church you attend as a family. Advent workshops, summer camps, Vacation Bible School—all need helpers. Imagine the impact you would make on your stepchildren by volunteering for a program they're a part of.

Having a strong and certain walk with the Lord yourself is, of course, the most important way to model the Christian life, the Spirit-led life. If your stepchildren see you pray, they're more likely to pray too. If you attend church with them, they will be more interested in going. If they know you turn to God with your problems and petitions and praises, they'll feel the freedom to do the same.

If they hear you ask forgiveness of God and of those you've hurt—including them at times—they'll more readily do the same and be willing to share with others the joy that results from a clean heart.

Darlene Riggan said she remembers the day her stepfather became a Christian. Later he taught her the Lord's Prayer and what it meant—line by line. As an adult, Darlene realized that her stepfather was the person who most influenced her spiritually. "Pop was a devout Christian who truly walked the walk in his daily life," said Darlene. "We attended church regularly. And I remember how he liked having me play hymns on the piano where he joined me in song. I miss him terribly."

Be an Adviser

Teenage and young adult stepchildren often turn to their stepparents as advisers, sometimes before they turn to their birth parents. A stepmother or stepfather can be an invaluable source of strength and support during a personal trial, an upset with a natural parent, or the death of a loved one.

Young people are also curious about your childhood and youth. What did you do in this or that situation? "What would you do?" they may ask. Be ready to share. Sometimes an advisor is more of a listener than anything else.

One stepdad said he found that he was at his best when he let his stepchildren talk out their troubles, and then he followed with a similar example and a decision from his own life. "I believe they learn more from what we do than from what we say," he added.

I was always inspired when my husband, Charles, shared stories from his life with my children. He helped my teenage son see the value of persevering in a business venture when he wanted to quit. He comforted my youngest daughter when her boyfriend walked out on her. He was able to relate to the situation because he remembered the pain he felt when a girl he thought he loved broke up with him.

Open sharing and listening can do so much to build the kind of lasting relationship that will impact stepchildren for their entire lives, not just for a day or a week or during a summer visit.

Be a Teacher

Stepparents make excellent teachers. They can partner with their spouses to teach the children values and skills and to lead the way when an important decision is pending. Often a stepparent can step back and take the long view at a time when the birth parent is too involved emotionally.

Jim said he used his gardening hobby to teach his stepchildren some essential lessons about the cycle of life and death and the importance of caring for living creatures who are dependent. Taking care of a pet can accomplish a similar purpose. Children are eager students, but they need a mature, loving adult to inspire them to take the lessons to heart and to apply them to their lives.

Actually, all parents are teachers whether or not they choose to be. Ask any child! Or better yet, observe children. They pattern their behavior after the significant people in their lives.

Be a Confidante

"I can tell my stepmother anything," said 13-year-old Maria. "Even if I got in trouble at school, she'd help me."

Who wouldn't love to receive such an acknowledgment? Children and teens today live in a troubled, uncertain world. They need not only solid friends outside the family but also at least one true confidante—someone they can be completely real with, a person who can handle the truth about them without freaking out. The child who can confide in a stepparent as well as a parent is blessed indeed.

How about your stepchildren? Do they feel safe with you? Can they tell you anything and trust that you won't turn away? Can they count on you to provide stability and strength during a crisis? It may be that you'll never have to accept this much responsibility, but if you do, are you ready and willing?

Being a stepparent is a lot more than being the spouse of the children's mother or father. The ideal stepparent is someone who wants to be a pal, a playmate, a friend, a spiritual model, an adviser, a teacher, and a confidante to the children and young people entrusted to his or her care.

BUILDING A STRONG ONE-ON-ONE RELATIONSHIP

1. What new insight about your role as stepparent did you gain from this chapter? How might you apply what you learned to your life?

2. What new aspect of your stepparenting role would you like to explore (playmate, pal, teacher, spiritual model, and so on)? What practical steps could you take to put this into action?

3. Based on what you read in this chapter, write down three ways you could foster more intimacy and closeness between you and your stepchildren.

PART 2

Step by Step:
Memories Are
Made of This

4
Making Memories
That Matter

MOST OF US THINK OF PARENTS, grandparents, aunts, uncles, and friends as memory-makers. But what about stepparents? They can create memorable moments too.

Eric McNew of Edmond, Oklahoma, said he expanded his parenting years by 10 when he married again after his first wife died and his youngest went off to college.

"I had to shift gears," he said. "I had to change my mental attitude from 'just the two of us' to being a stepdad to a teenage boy who didn't want one and a little girl who was hoping and praying for a daddy."

The children's father, Steve, had died of cancer after being confined to a wheelchair following a brain injury that resulted from being hit by a teenaged drunk driver.

"One part of me wanted to run as far away as fast as I could," Eric admitted. "But another part was drawn to these two sweet kids who needed a godly male role model in their home."

Eric said he wrestled in prayer over the decision to marry. "I was 49 years old, and I resisted the 'assignment' of starting again with a 10-year-old and parenting for ten more years."

But Eric knew he wouldn't be happy unless he was doing what God wanted. "I believe this was where I was needed most," he said.

Right from the start, Eric began making memories—but

they had a negative effect! He continually reminded his wife, Cyndi, to discipline the kids for behavior he felt was unacceptable. It took a Christian counselor and the Holy Spirit, Eric claims, to show him that he had to stop what he was doing.

Eric turned to God in prayer. He knew he couldn't be the stepfather he wanted to be without the help of the Holy Spirit.

"I began calling out the names of my three children and my two stepchildren," he said. *"O God,* I prayed, *change in Tate and Katelyn what I cannot change.* It was amazing what I began to see, especially in Katelyn."

He also encouraged his wife, Cyndi, to continue to wear the wedding ring from her marriage to her first husband, and he would wear his wedding ring from his marriage to his first wife—as a way to honor the memory of their children's deceased parents. He didn't want the kids to think the two of them were putting away their real mom and dad. "I consider this visual symbol to be special and meaningful," Eric added.

He is also known for getting down on the floor and playing with the kids—from Barbie dolls with Katelyn to monsters in the swimming pool or going on rides with her at the amusement park.

Eric seems especially sensitive to preserving the memory of the children's father, giving them total freedom to talk about him any time they wish. "I want them to be able to express their grief and loss and how much they miss their dad without its being perceived as a threat to me."

Eric's situation is unique to him, just as mine is to me and yours is to you. We can support one another, however, by finding out what others do. Consider some of the ways you can make positive memories with your stepchildren.

Share top-quality time together. It will multiply.

Find out what each stepchild likes to do, and build that activity or event into your routine together. For example, whenever my stepdaughter, Cathy, visited her dad and me, she enjoyed shopping at the mall, helping her father in his real estate business, going out for lunch or dinner, and walking along the beach near our home.

You don't have to work at these activities. Let them emerge as you get to know one another and find common interests. When you enjoy being together in a meaningful way, you'll be building memories that last, and you'll all want to repeat them whenever you're together.

And what about sharing time with adult stepchildren? How can you do that successfully without making demands on their lives?

Sandy Peckham wondered at first how she could build strong one-on-one relationships with her two stepchildren, who were in their 20s when she married their father.

"Because I didn't have children of my own, I wanted the four of us to be a close family," said Sandy. "Naturally that didn't happen as quickly as I had hoped, partly because my stepchildren were already living on their own."

Sandy worried that she would never make a positive difference in their lives. "Because they were grown, I thought it was too late. They were exploring the work world and seeking spouses of their own. They had little interest in me, their dad's wife."

She admitted fighting off feelings of disappointment, rejection, and self-pity. "Like the psalmist, I carried my deepest feelings to the Lord, and I began to pray. Night after night, month after month, I asked Him to bond us. I came to understand that one of the most influential things I could do for my stepchildren was to pray."

Sandy said she had to quell her personal longing to be their heroine and instead pursue God's path for building a relationship with them, a path that began alone with God on her knees. "I waited and I kept praying," she said.

Four years later, Sandy mentioned to her husband that she would like the children and their spouses to join them at the beach for a weekend. "He loved the idea," she said, "and he praised me for having such a loving suggestion. This would be the first time in our marriage that all of us would be together around the clock. We found a weekend that worked for the six of us. It turned out to be Father's Day weekend. Unknown to my husband, I began planning a surprise.

"I implemented the idea of a 'Tree of Love' from the book *Let's Make a Memory,* by Gloria Gaither and Shirley Dobson. I sent a letter to my stepchildren explaining the idea. They were to write four or five reasons why they loved their father or write about a special memory of their dad. My stepchildren's spouses participated too." They spent two days together, eating, talking, walking on the beach, playing miniature golf, swimming, shopping, and laughing together.

"The weekend came to a close, and my stepson clandestinely handed me the signed slips of paper. I rolled each slip into a scroll. Then, following breakfast, I tied the scrolls to a small branch anchored in a clay pot and placed it in the center of the dining table."

For the next hour, Sandy's husband unrolled each scroll and read aloud the reasons his children, their mates, and his wife loved him.

"Some reasons were humorous, and some were serious, but all were touching," said Sandy. "My husband cried, I cried, and his children had the opportunity to honor their father in a way we'll never forget.

"After that time of tender transparency and sharing, we gathered in the living room overlooking the gentle ocean waves to worship as a family. Prior to the trip I had selected some praise and worship songs, printed the words on song sheets, and asked my stepson, who plays the guitar, to lead our singing.

"All I can say is that the Lord was there. He was with us that day and the entire weekend."

Later Sandy said she was able to see and experience a bond with her stepchildren. She had the courage to take a risk and obey God's prompting, and He answered her prayers. Will He do any less for you and me?

Share a little money. It will come back to you.

Most kids don't have the freedom to spend unlimited amounts of money as they please. As a stepparent, you may have a say in how your stepchildren learn to understand and use money in a responsible way. You and your spouse will likely supervise their purchases or advise them about how to use the money they receive or earn.

As a stepparent, however, you may be able to offer an occasional "treat" without crossing established boundaries. For example, suppose your spouse and your stepchild's other natural parent take care of the child's basic needs. Maybe you could offer to cover music or art lessons. This could be a respectful way for you to participate in the financial area of your stepchild's life—but only if you want to.

Or you might want to start a special savings account for a designated purpose. As you become involved in whatever way is acceptable to the children's parents, you have the opportunity to share with your stepchildren some of the principles of wise earning, spending, saving, comparison shopping, and so on. You needn't be heavy-handed about it. But be ready to respond in a helpful way when you have the chance.

Consider giving your stepchildren a couple of dollars (or more, depending on their ages) to spend as they wish when they go shopping with you. Or tuck a dollar into an envelope with a note inviting them to buy a little treat on you. And of course, it would be important to allow for trial and error. That's how they'll learn. The more conservative stepchild might put the money into the bank for a future purchase. The spontaneous one is likely to buy the first thing he or she sees and then regret it. However they choose to respond, allow them to learn from it without adding your judgments or opinions.

You can help out financially in other ways too. One stepmom is paying for baseball uniforms for her two stepsons who live with their single mother. The two women have a cordial relationship that allows the stepmother to make such a gift without its being a problem for the boys' mother.

My ex-husband and his wife provide an opportunity each summer for my children to go to Catalina Island with them for two weeks. This tradition has been such a happy experience for everyone that they're carrying it over to the next generation. Now my grandchildren are enjoying the same blessing.

Share your energy. Why save it?

One man I know became a stepfather at age 55. He married a woman 20 years his junior who had two sons. Richard was concerned about keeping up with these energetic seven- and nine-year-old boys. He was in love with their mother but not sure he wanted active young children running through their home. He didn't like surprises, he liked to observe rather than participate, and he often stayed behind when there was an outing on the calendar.

Certainly there's room in the Stepparents' Club for people of every personality type and style—even couch potatoes—but those who are dedicated nonparticipators generally miss out on the love, the fun, the traditions, and the joy of making memories with their stepchildren. If you're one who's tempted to skip outings with your family, consider the fact that you'll never pass this way again—and neither will your stepchildren.

Share your creativity. And watch it pop up in your stepchildren.

Laura is an amateur photographer and stepmother of two adolescent girls who visit Laura and their dad every other weekend. Laura admits that she and Betsy and Margie had some problems. She felt uncomfortable in her own home when they were around. She knew, however, that it was up to her to bridge the chasm between them. They hadn't wanted their parents to divorce, and they hadn't wanted their father to remarry. She couldn't expect from them anything more than she was willing to do herself.

So as Laura put it, "I rolled up my sleeves and got to work

to make the girls a priority in my life. I knew I would not have a happy marriage if my husband's children weren't happy with me—or at least accepting. I wanted to reach them. I decided to share my interest and see what might happen."

Laura gave each stepdaughter a camera for Christmas the first year they visited. Now the girls look forward to this special connection with Laura. They've created photo memory albums together and have something unique to talk about when they're together. "It's opened a new world to all of us," Laura said.

Share your knowledge. Watch it take root.

Fourteen-year-old Martin is a Civil War enthusiast largely because of his stepfather's passion for that period in United States history. Even as a young boy, he listened to his stepdad tell stories about the rivalry between the Confederates and the Yankees and how his home state of Kentucky tried to remain neutral and ended up hated by both sides.

Martin and his stepdad subscribe to *Kentucky Explorer Magazine* and the History Book Club, sharing books and articles on Civil War-related topics. They've traveled together as a family to some of the famous battle sites, and Martin has enjoyed the benefit of his stepfather's expertise while he was researching a topic for a history project on the Civil War.

What a privilege it is for Martin to have access to such knowledge! But it doesn't stop there. Some of the things his stepfather knows originated with an ancestor who served in the Confederacy during the Civil War. Martin not only has a partner to share his interest, but he's also learning something about his stepfather's family tree. What a gift! Imagine what a memory and tradition that will be for Martin and his own children someday.

Share your own history. Give your stepchildren a sense of their roots.

About 15 years ago my husband and I put together a framed collage of photos from a visit with his daughter,

Cathy. Whenever I look at it, memories of that time together come back.

At another time while visiting my sister's home for a family reunion, my youngest daughter, now an adult, pulled out some of the old photo albums piled on the living room floor. As she leafed through one after another, Charles and I enjoyed watching her reactions and listening to her comments as she recalled first one event and then another from her childhood—both before and after her dad and I separated.

Of course, she would have preferred for her natural parents to stay together, as most children would. But she also acknowledged how different life would be for all of us without Charles, her stepdad. Even her children see the abundance he has brought to our family life. To them he's not merely a distant "step" relative.

Charles deserves credit for much of the affection our family feels toward him. He has participated in his stepchildren's lives in an active way, and he has shared his family (parents, brother, sister-in-law, and nephew) with us.

Together we've displayed our family heritage in what we've dubbed "The Family Museum." It has stimulated many questions and comments.

"Where did you get that beautiful old quilt? It looks handmade," said one of my friends as she paused in front of the glass doors of the old cherry wood bookcase that stands in the entry hall of our home. "And look at those lovely silver spoons and the Fostoria serving set. My grandmother had one just like it. And that old Bible. And the Shirley Temple drinking cup. What treasures!"

As you can tell, we display quite a few heirlooms in our home. Some years ago as we were packing and unpacking boxes during a move, we paused to look at all the items that had been passed down through the generations in our families: real china play dishes that were nearly a century old, my husband's first metronome from his childhood piano-playing days, his father's railroad pocket watch, a dictionary my grandfather had given me on my eighth birthday—and many more items of great personal value.

Charles suggested we select as many treasures as our bookcase could artfully hold, clean them up, and put them on display. The books could go on a shelf in the den. But our heirlooms, many of them priceless to us, should be set out for friends and family to enjoy.

Today our collection is also a living museum as we periodically add small, special things that represent our ongoing lives: a yarn doll we bought in Mexico, a crèche set made in Germany, our children's first shoes. Most important, however, our museum serves as an anchor to the past. It reminds us of people and events that can't be replaced or duplicated—especially in the lives of our sons and daughters and now our grandchildren. And it's been a special tool for our stepchildren to get to know us in a new way.

If such a custom interests you, it's easy to get started. Ask your parents or other living relatives for photos, shoes, trinkets, coins, spoons, cups, old books, a glass water pitcher, or other items that have special meaning to your family. Such things may already be in your possession or in the attic, basement, or closet.

Chances are that your relatives would be proud and pleased to share them with you. My mother was so flattered when I asked her to save me one of my grandmother's hand-painted ice-cream dishes that she gave me the entire set on the spot!

Place your treasured items on a shelf where they'll be easily seen, or buy or make a cabinet with glass doors for a permanent and safe display. Make your collection as personal as you wish. It can be a tribute to the past, a living memory of current times, or a blend of the two—a testimony to your individual and family connections.

Tip: Put a sticker on the bottom of each treasure or heirloom in your family museum with the name of the person you wish to leave it to after you're gone. Make a master list, and keep it with your important papers, such as your will.

Share your memories of your stepchildren. What a gift!

Some stepparents—particularly those who live full-time with their stepchildren—keep track of their lives together through a journal, a running letter to each child to be given to him or her when he or she leaves home, photo albums, or a similar item.

Darlene Riggan said she has received wonderful acknowledgment from her adult stepchildren for the way she has documented their lives. "It if weren't for Darlene," one said, "we would have no memory of our childhood."

Photography is one of Darlene's passions, and she takes pictures or videos of every major event. Following a family cruise, for example, she made a calendar—highlighting the birthdays and anniversaries in each month—with pictures from the trip.

As a stepparent, you, too, may wish to create a keepsake for your stepchildren. What are your special memories of the various stages of their lives? How would you like to bring those memories to life for yourself and for them? Here are some ideas others have used successfully.

• *Memories on tape.* You can record your thoughts, feelings, and reflections on audiocassette or videocassette. Make recordings during momentous occasions, after a visit together, or following an event you attended with them, such as a music recital, athletic event, family holiday, or at any other time you feel like expressing yourself to your stepchildren. You could present these as gifts each year or compile several and give them on special occasions. Imagine how your stepchild will feel to receive such a personal present.

Darlene has drawn on her own experience as a stepchild, and her effort has helped her stepchildren appreciate her even more.

"My stepfather died in 1998," she said, "and just before his death I learned the value of telling him how much he meant to me. Father's Day was later in the same month, so I suggested a special 'Tribute to Fathers' and asked each family member to come to our celebration with a memory to share as a tribute to his or her father. My husband and I wrote tributes to our fathers, the children and stepchildren to theirs, and our grandchildren to their fathers. I made a video for each one of us—something we'll all treasure forever."

• *Memories on paper.* One stepparent keeps a written record of his precious moments with his only child—his stepdaughter, Katrina. Each event or experience they share is kept in the form of a letter. He tells Katrina his thoughts, feelings, observations, and remembrances about her. Sometimes he gives her a letter as a gift for a birthday or holiday. "But I always keep a copy in a box here at home," he said. "That way, when I'm gone she'll have a whole set."

I've written personal notes to my stepchildren—even as adults—for birthdays and Christmas or after memorable times together.

• *Memories in a scrapbook.* You can do this project together with your stepchildren. When they reach school age, help them assemble important papers, documents, photos, ribbons, awards, and so on, in a scrapbook. Add captions and comments, and be sure to date the entries.

I'm not a stepchild, but one of my aunts—a kind of stepmom to me in her own way—compiled a photo album of snapshots of me throughout my life and captioned each page with a line from the famous poem "She Walks in Beauty," by Lord Byron. This was her wedding gift to me. I still have the album—a visual history of my life as well as a scrapbook of memories.

• *Memories on a wall.* Ellen has lined the stairway walls of her Minnesota home with photo collages of children and stepchildren. At a glance, one can see the people, places, and events that make up the fabric of her family. She's a widow now, so the "memory wall," as she calls it, brings her special comfort and joy. It includes pictures that span several decades, providing family members with a visual history of their heritage from great-great-grandparents and aunts and uncles and cousins to contemporary relatives who live in various parts of the world.

Whatever way you choose to make memories and build traditions, the important thing is that you do something. If all these ideas seem overwhelming, pick out just one to start. Look at some of the things that were meaningful to you as a child—whether or not you had stepparents. What memories and traditions do you treasure? You may wish to start a similar tradition with your children and stepchildren.

If the adults in your life were passive about such things, then you have all the more reason to change that pattern in your relationship with your stepchildren.

Time is short. Kids grow up quickly. Take action now to make memories and build traditions with your stepchildren that will enrich and deepen their lives and bless yours as well. And remember: there's no one way to do any of this. The idea is to select what's comfortable and appropriate for your relationship with your stepchild or stepchildren.

Cyndi and Eric McNew have displayed their memories on one wall in their home. Wedding photos of Eric and his former wife, Debbie, hang on the left, and Cyndi and Steve on their wedding day are on the right. Eric and Cyndi have placed their own wedding photo in the middle. "I see this as another way to honor the memories of the kids' deceased parents," said Eric.

BUILDING A STRONG ONE-ON-ONE RELATIONSHIP

1. Choose one practical tool you received from this chapter, and write a simple plan for implementing it in your relationship with your stepchildren. (For example: Start a journal for each stepchild, recording your impressions and feelings as he or she is growing up. Purchase a small blank book or loose-leaf notebook for each child.)

2. Think of one tradition that your parents or stepparents introduced you to as a child. How might you resurrect that with your stepchildren so they'll sense the links between generations? (For example, each Christmas maybe you and your family made fudge from scratch—a recipe handed down from a grandmother. You could introduce your stepchildren to this tradition.)

3. Consider something that's important to you in your life today. How could you pass that on to your stepchildren? (For example: If you're a music or theater enthusiast, introduce your stepchildren to these experiences by taking them to a concert or ballet or stage play a couple of times a year. If you like to hike or fish or surf, take them along when they reach the appropriate age, and teach them your skill.)

5
Just the Two of You

ONCE MANY YEARS AGO I WENT to New York City to speak at a writers' conference. My stepdaughter, Cathy, lived on Long Island at the time, so I invited her to meet me for lunch at the hotel where I was staying. Then we walked the streets of New York City, window shopping and talking. It was a simple get-together, but it meant a lot to both of us.

"I like being with you," she said. "There's always something exciting going on."

What a blessing it was to hear such a spontaneous display of affection! It was just the two of us—having fun, drawing closer as we walked and talked.

My daughter Erin has similar warm feelings about my husband, Charles, her stepfather. Recently we visited her and her family to help them settle into their new home. Charles brought his tool kit, his oldest jeans, and his beat-up tennis shoes. He was ready to work in the yard and around the house wherever she needed him. He pulled out old shrubs and drooping ivy, trimmed overgrown bushes, and raked and shoveled loads of dirt. Then the two of them drove to the garden shop and bought a few flats of flowers to plant.

There they were—Erin, age 35, and Charles, age 73—just the two of them together. Whether you're in a relationship with toddlers, teens, or grown adults, you're a vital part of your stepchildren's lives, and I can't imagine anything more special than top-quality time together—for a chore, an errand, an outing, a meal—as long as you make sure that from time to time it's just the two of you.

When younger stepchildren are with you for a visit, a long stay, or everyday living, one of the best investments you can make is spending time alone together. A stop at the dollar store or the whale exhibit at the museum of natural history, a tour of a horse farm, or a walk through the mall or the local park can be extra special when you don't have to share that time with anyone else.

Remember, though, that you don't have to leave home to make something special happen for the two of you. Building with Legos on the floor, tossing a ball in the backyard, digging weeds out of the front lawn, baking a chocolate cake together—are all ways to draw close, to talk, to listen, to find out more about one another without the distraction of others around you.

A COUPLE OF PALS

People of all ages are hungry for undivided personal time with one of their loved ones. Husbands and wives want more time alone with one another. Kids want to feel special to each parent, and most parents and stepparents want to connect with the children in a personal way. But somehow life—the daily routine, what I call the "have tos"—gets in the way.

There's work and laundry and grocery shopping and school and Little League and piano lessons and PTA meetings and church and Sunday School and—well, you know how it goes. Weeks and months slip by to the point where some families feel that waving hello and good-bye is the extent of their contact.

But stepparents have the unique opportunity to take the kids *out* for a quality "just-the-two-of-us" visit. It doesn't require money or even much time. It does require, however, that you *be* there, present to the child as a person who cares, who listens, who empathizes, who affirms, who is fun, who is easy to be with. That can take place over a pancake breakfast at a neighborhood café or during a shared moment at a symphony or football game.

Whatever you choose, make sure it's something for just the two of you. By the way, sitting on a bench reading a newspaper while your stepchild plays alone in the sand at the park is not what I'm talking about. Dropping off your stepchild at a library event for kids and picking him or her up later doesn't count either!

Just the two of you means just that—you and your stepchild together, interacting, doing something specific, or just hanging out, walking and talking.

For example, Eric McNew and his stepdaughter, Katelyn, celebrated their first stepdaughter-stepfather Father's Day in a special way. "I walked in wearing a tuxedo and carrying a long-stemmed rose," said Eric. "'Put on your fanciest dress and fix your hair,' I told Katelyn. 'I'm taking you out in my Corvette.'"

Eric took her to one of the most elegant restaurants in their town—Nikz, on top of Founder's Tower in Edmond, Oklahoma, near Oklahoma City—the one with a revolving floor and a great view of the city in lights at night.

He also left a note for his stepson Tate then aged 15, telling him what he and Katelyn were doing on the Saturday before Father's Day. He invited Tate to set a date when the two of them could have a stepfather-stepson celebration at the same restaurant.

"I had not come into their lives to replace their father," said Eric. "In fact, I told Jeremy, my older stepson who was in college and who really didn't need me in his life, that I knew their dad was irreplaceable. I only hoped that one day as Jer filed past my casket, he might say, 'I loved Eric because he loved my mom so much, treated her like a queen, and was good to my younger brother and sister.'"

STEPPARENT CALENDAR

If you want to have a strong one-on-one relationship with your stepchildren, I believe it's essential to find ways to interact with them, as Eric talked about, one at a time. Following are some possibilities to consider:

• Ask your stepchild to help you paint a room, set the table, plant flowers, or mow the grass.

• Invite one at a time on different days to go out for a quick meal or to visit a museum or library for a couple of hours.

• Sign up for a class with one of your older stepchildren. This is a great way to spend time together in a meaningful way. It will stir up conversation and draw you into projects where you can share ideas. Loretta and Jeannie are both creative, so they took a cake-decorating class together.

• Combine business and pleasure. For example, you could take one of your stepchildren on a short trip or invite him or her to attend a conference with you where there might be activities for family members. My brother often takes his oldest son to the National Speakers Association yearly conventions. My nephew is learning more about his dad's profession as well as participating in some educational opportunities in public speaking for young people. This experience also gives them time alone to talk and share and just be together.

Nancy, a schoolteacher I met, said her stepdaughter helps her get her classroom ready each September. She decorates the bulletin boards and stacks the textbooks. "It's a time for us to chat, to be together, and have fun. I know this experience has influenced her to consider being a teacher herself someday," said Nancy.

These events all take some planning—no doubt about that. Is it worth it? You bet. You'll be able to see for yourself when you look at the expression in your stepchild's eyes, when you see a change in his or her behavior toward you, when you talk about things the two of you have shared.

Marcia Ramsland, professional organizer from San Diego, suggests that parents and stepparents use a daily planner to stay on task and to keep appointments and promises—not only for the fun stuff but also for running a household effectively. She encourages families to work *together* so everyone has an investment in how the home is managed and maintained. This, too, is a way to build intimacy.

Marcia has a system she's trademarked as "The Two-Minute Pickup," which she shared with me recently.

Here's how it works. Before you leave your house for work, school, church, a meeting, an outing, ask each family member to do one of the following. Each step takes just two minutes or less.

1. Send an E-mail or make a phone call that moves an action forward. (Call ahead for restaurant reservations or concert tickets, for example.)
2. Return books, toys, and clothes to their proper drawer, closet, or cabinet. (Everyone can do his or her share with this.)
3. Make your bed, dust the furniture in one room, stack the dirty dishes in the dishwasher.
4. Clear off and wipe down your desk, countertop, or kitchen table.
5. Organize tools or equipment needed for your next project upon your return. (For example, lay out clothes for the following day, prepare necessary items to complete a homework assignment, set the table for the next meal, and so on).
6. Start a load of laundry, or fold a few items that have already been washed and sorted.
7. Water the plants. Feed the dog. Put the cat out.

"It's not the things we do that make us tired," said Marcia. "It's the things left undone that wear us out. Fragmentation causes fatigue, while a clean and organized space energizes you for the entire day! It also contributes to healthy and happy relationships. Control is not a once-and-for-all experience. It is steadily practiced and gained each day through good habits." And it's something everyone can achieve. Stepparents, lead the way!

We can't afford to rely on happenstance. Between the kids' sports and school activities and your work life, nothing will happen if you don't plan ahead. With a "Stepparent Calendar" in place—even if you keep it private—you're more likely to carry out what you want and hope to do. Writing down a plan or a date and getting the other person's agreement will propel you into action. Like everything else in life, we have to get our ideas, dreams, hopes, and wishes underway with a bit of strategic and *advance* planning.

Sometimes those who have the fullest schedules accomplish more of what they want because they have to plan in order to meet their goals.

IDEAS FOR JUST THE TWO OF YOU

Infants and Babies

Hold them, rock them, read to them, sing to them, or use a stroller or baby carriage for a walk.

Toddlers and Preschoolers

Play with blocks, building equipment, and toys. Read books, swim, run, take a nature walk and point out flowers and insects, bake or cook something simple and fun. One stepmother said she and her young stepdaughter enjoy making finger sandwiches with cookie cutters. They cut the bread into various shapes, such as hearts, stars, and circles, and then they spread jam and peanut butter or cream cheese on matching halves. This is great for a party or picnic.

Primary Grade Children

When they visit overnight or are with you for an extended stay (holidays or summer vacation), plan some simple but special activities you can do together: bake cookies or muffins; go swimming; visit the library or museum; attend a puppet show or stage play for children. Give them a dollar or two to spend however they want at a variety store. Make a picnic lunch together, and eat at the park or beach.

Youth and Preteens

Boys and girls between 8 and 12 years of age enjoy some of the same activities listed for primary grade children, but you can expand the experiences to meet their ages and interest levels. For example, these children might like to enroll in a program at a park, whereas a younger child may be content with a shorter play time at the park.

Older children may also enjoy cooking projects and, unlike the younger ones, could actually help you fix an entire meal. They also like to have gift money to spend as they wish. From time to time, ask what they would do with $5, $10, or $50. You'll find out their interests and preferences this way and get some ideas for birthday and Christmas gifts.

For example, one boy wanted a telescope and a book about the stars. He didn't care about anything else. No one in the family knew he was that interested in astronomy, but he was. It was a secret desire. He received the telescope and book last year and is still pursuing his hobby. It was not merely a passing fancy.

In fact, shopping for a large, wanted gift item such as a telescope, camera, laptop computer, and so on is a great way to spend time with an older stepchild. For example, if you offer to buy a bicycle or musical instrument or to pay for two weeks of summer camp, you could research the purchase or the project together. Consider the learning and the intimacy that would come from such a venture.

If you decide to vacation as a family and include stepchildren who may not live with you full time, draw them into the planning phase. Put each one in charge of something. Look at maps and travel guides, research the Internet, and create an itinerary that includes activities that everyone will enjoy.

One of my friends took her only stepson to Europe with her when he was 12 years old. She let him take his in-line skates along. She likes to bicycle, so the two of them had a great time rolling along the paths and roads of France and Holland. Depending on the age of your stepchildren, your financial means, and the time involved, you may wish to plan a similar trip. If you're not up for biking or skating, how about a walking or hiking tour? Or a cruise? Or a camping trip?

If you're a less active person, so be it. All it really takes is two people spending time together in a way that pleases them both. This can include a strenuous activity, a mild activity, or no activity at all—as long as you're with each other.

Teens and Young Adults

Stepchildren in the teen-to-young-adult age group frequently have busy lives of their own, and it may be more difficult to reach them for private visits, but you can still make the effort. They'll appreciate your desire to stay connected. By the time they reach high school, they may enjoy a dinner or theater date with you, a short trip to a destination they help choose, or your presence at one of their games, concerts, or other high school or college events.

If they're deliberating which college to attend, you can help them research various schools, offering your advice and experience. Then visit them at college and stay close through letters and phone calls.

One day Eric McNew stumbled upon the fact that his college-age stepson Jeremy looked forward to receiving mail while away from home. "Right then I saw an opportunity," Eric said, "a need I could fill."

From that point on, Eric began writing to Jeremy weekly, passing on funny stories or comments, sending photos of the family, and throwing in some godly advice from time to time. The two have developed a great friendship. "I often talk with him about spiritual issues," said Eric, "including a healthy outlook toward sexual matters and the temptations all men face."

One day when Jeremy came home on break, Eric threw him the keys to his prized Corvette, and said simply, "Have fun!"

Today one of Eric's fondest memories is the day Jeremy and his fiancé asked Eric to perform their wedding ceremony.

The consistent presence of a caring stepparent in the life of a child from the time you meet and into adulthood is a blessing that can't be measured.

More Ideas for Just the Two of You

Following is a collection of ideas that stepparents have shared with me. You can choose those that interest you and match them appropriately with your stepchildren.

• **Start a hobby together.** Collect stamps, teacups, bottle caps, or greeting cards. Join a bird-watching club. Paint or sketch together.

• **Volunteer for public service.** Feed the homeless. Pick up trash in a local park. Help with a political campaign. Plant greenery along the streets in your community. Collect glass and newspapers from neighbors, and take them to the recycling center.

• **Take your stepchild to work with you.** Give him or her a behind-the-scenes tour of your office or place of business. Introduce your stepchild to coworkers, and give him or her a chance to ask questions or to try out a process or activity associated with your work—providing it's safe and all right with management.

• **Put together a family recipe book.** You can gather recipes from both sides of the family. Ask aunts, uncles, or cousins to share their favorites, and include your own as well.

• **Participate in the church choir, a skit, Vacation Bible School, community play, or family camp together.** Even though you'll be with other people, the experience of just the two of you, as opposed to you and all the members of your family, will be special.

• **Plant a flower or vegetable garden together.** If you don't have a yard, you can create a window garden. Perhaps you could start one at each of your homes if you don't live together full time and then help each other keep the gardens going and growing.

• **Plan a surprise for a member of the family.** You and one of your stepchildren could fix a special meal or plan an activity for the other parent or a sibling—one that no one knows about but the two of you. This is a good opportunity for you to be together for a common purpose.

Building a Strong One-on-One Relationship

1. Consider the ideas mentioned in this chapter. Depending on the ages of your stepchildren and where they live in relation to you, which ideas can you use now, and which could you use in the future? Naturally, you can do more things with those who are close by than those who live far away.

2. Make a stepparent calendar. Depending on how many stepchildren you have and their ages, plan specific ways for you to spend time alone with each one during the course of the year. Consult their natural parents, if that's customary, so you can coordinate your schedules. You may have to make some adjustments along the way, but with ideas in writing, you're likely to accomplish most, if not all, of the plans you make.

3. Ask each of your stepchildren to tell you or give you a list of ways he or she would like to spend time with you. You might be surprised and delighted by the suggestions. Act on the ones that are appropriate. And whatever you do, remember to do it with a sense of joy rather than obligation.

6
Stepparenting Around the Block or Across the Country

ROBIN'S STEPCHILDREN—A 10-YEAR-OLD BOY and a 7-year-old girl—lived with Robin and their dad from the time she married their father. The children's mother had died the year before, so Robin had a big role to fill.

Dan, on the other hand, lives miles away from his teenaged stepson, Alex, who lives in another state with his natural father. Dan sees Alex only a couple of times a year over Christmas vacation and for a month each summer. He has no children of his own, though he has always wanted to be a father some day. Therefore, his relationship with Alex is important to him. And he knows it means a lot to his wife for him to take an interest in her son.

Dan writes to Alex by E-mail a few times a month and phones occasionally just to say hi and find out how he's doing. He knows his wife has regular conversations with Alex as well, and he could tag on to those phone calls.

"Some people might think it's strange for me to go to such extremes to keep up with the boy—especially since he has a father he's close to—but I really like Alex. We have a lot in common. I've never tried to take his father's place. We both know I'm mostly an older friend."

Dan said Alex's dad approves of their friendship. Maybe that's because Dan has been up-front about it. I admire him for taking the time to get to know Alex and then pursuing a relationship. Dan admits their visits are a lot more enjoyable because of the E-mail and phone contact they have during the rest of the year.

"We don't have to start fresh each time we're together," he said, "and my wife really appreciates this. She doesn't worry about my feeling left out or jealous that Alex is taking up most of her time during his visits."

Dan says that during their times together he feels they really are a family. "It's good for all of us," he says.

Dan and Alex are probably the exception, but they need not be. Any adult who wishes to make a lasting contribution to a stepchild—whether the boy or girl lives near or far away—can do so. It's a matter of willingness and follow-through.

It takes more effort to be a stepparent across the miles than to be one down the street or in the next town. But we can do it if we want to. After hearing Dan's story, I know how worthwhile it is.

And what about the benefits for us, the stepparents? Only each one of us knows the answer to that question. My hunch is that it's just as important for us to be friends with our stepchildren as it is for them to become friends with us. But to bring this about, you must make it happen. The following are some ideas that other long-distance stepparents have shared.

Calling All Stepchildren

The telephone is an obvious first thought. You can talk to your stepchildren nearly anywhere in the world. Then again, maybe you can't do it easily. Depending on the time difference, the people involved, and their locations, it may take some planning.

Most of us today, including children, have access to E-mail. This isn't quite as personal as the phone (hearing each other's voice is the best way to stay connected), but it's a wonderful second best choice.

Following are some suggestions for making the most of your telephone calls and E-mails.

Plan your calls. Find out your stepchildren's routines—

school hours, meals, bedtimes, weekend activities, church, and so on. Some stepparents pick up the phone at their own convenience only and then wonder why they sometimes get a poor reception or the call is cut short.

Avoid small talk. "How's the weather? We're having a downpour here."

"What have you been up to?"

"Sure is hard to nail you down. Seems you're gone most of the time."

Awkward passages like these would never even occur to a stepparent who knows what the stepchildren are doing at school and in their leisure time, remembers the names of some of their best friends, shares a hobby or interest such as music, sewing, skiing, or stamp collecting, understands where the stepchildren are spiritually, or recalls important dates and events in their lives.

If you have access to all this information, you'll have topics for many interesting phone conversations. To remain current, keep a note pad handy as you're speaking. Write down the names of their new friends and the date of the basketball tournament or the school play. Then you'll not only be prepared to call and ask how the event turned out but might also even send a fax or a bouquet of flowers to celebrate the occasion.

Talk about yourself. It's important to foster a two-way relationship. Let your stepchildren know the names of some of your friends and the important dates in your life. Ask the older ones for their advice or their perspective on something. For example, "What kind of sandwiches would a teenage youth group like? I'm in charge of refreshments," or "If you wanted a couple of days off work and you'd used up all your vacation time, how would you ask your boss for more? I could use a little help on this one."

Look forward to something together. If you see your stepchildren during the holidays or you're planning a trip to their town next summer, mention this on the phone. Let them participate in the planning. Depending on their age, you can

ask them to get information about a play you want to see with
them, a tour of a historic building, a side trip to the ocean, or
whatever. Notice how you and your stepchildren will draw
closer as you plan your visit and anticipate it together.

Rediscovering Letter Writing

In this age of technology, the art of letter writing may
seem a bit old-fashioned—to everyone except the recipient,
that is. Many of those who don't like to *write* letters are the
same people who love to *receive* letters.

I doubt there's a man or woman alive who doesn't enjoy
finding a personally addressed letter in the mailbox.
Stepchildren and stepparents are no different.

Picture this. Young Stacy flips through the afternoon mail
and spots your handwriting on the envelope addressed to
her. She'll probably call her best friend and tell her about it
right away.

A couple of weeks later (maybe sooner), it's you who gets
excited when you see Stacy's familiar handwriting on an envelope addressed to you. "Look at this," you may tell your
spouse. "A letter from Stacy. And she's enclosed her school
picture."

If you would like to revive the art of letter writing in your
family, here are some suggestions that may help.

Match your letter to the stepchild's age and experience. A
short one-page note in large bold print will delight toddlers
or preschoolers. Even if they can't read themselves, they'll be
thrilled by receiving mail and having it read to them. Add a
stick of chewing gum or a page of stickers for an even more
delightful surprise. Or how about a few computer graphics
that add color and humor to the page?

Lengthen your letters appropriately for older stepchildren.
Again, avoid small talk. If you know some facts about their
lives, their friends, and their activities, mention them. Ask
questions. Tell them you'll be pulling for their basketball
team to win or that you'll be praying for a good grade on a
spelling test.

Add a few details about your life, and ask for their prayers too. Be sure to end every letter by expressing your love. No one on the face of the earth can hear or read the words "I love you" too often. It's one way we can afford to thoroughly spoil one another—especially the children in our lives.

Create quick notes by keeping a stack of prestamped post-cards (available at the post office) in a handy place. This method of written correspondence is less personal than a letter, but it can be a good link between letters and phone calls. It can also take the place of a letter when you're in a hurry or on a trip.

Speed your correspondence over the miles with a fax if you and your stepchildren have access to a fax machine or computer fax program. You also can help a stepchild with homework, create a report, or generate a necessary response to some inquiry by using faxes to communicate. I don't believe this option takes the place of a mailed letter, but it still works.

Increase your chances of getting a reply by sending your stepchildren stationery or note cards as an occasional gift. Add a good ballpoint pen and a book of stamps, and they'll have no excuse not to write to you! One stepmom sent her college-bound stepdaughter a stack of stamped scenic postcards and a stamp pad that read, *Having a great time. Wish you were here. Love, Sally.*

"It worked," said her stepmother. "I think she got the message that I wanted to hear from her because I presented it in a playful way." Sally used the cards, and occasionally she even added a note of her own. Her stepmom was satisfied.

BUILDING A STRONG ONE-ON-ONE RELATIONSHIP

1. What one new thing will you do after reading this chapter?

2. Write a personal letter or send a card to each stepchild who lives across the miles.

3. Buy some postcards, stamp them, and keep them handy for quick notes.

PART 3
Stepping Up to the Changes and Challenges

7

What Your Stepchildren (Especially Teens) Really Need and Want From You

WHEN A TEEN'S NATURAL MOTHER and father both remarry, as was the case for my children, he or she must then find a rightful place in two blended families—which include stepparents, stepsiblings, stepgrandparents, and others on both sides. Building and managing all these relationships can result in stress for everyone—especially for teenagers who are already going through a volatile time in their own lives.

Once Charles and I were married and experienced some of the challenges, we took in all the information we could gather—the experiences of friends, their encouragement, and their advice. We also read books, listened to tapes, and attended personality and communication workshops. We knew we were in for the ride of our lives, and we wanted to hang on for the duration.

BAILING OUT

Eric McNew said he faced a huge challenge of his own and often felt like bailing out. "The hardest thing I've ever had to do for my stepkids is move into *their* house," he said. "Although every book advises against it, I believed I should do it, because the house was only three years old and was built with money received from the children's father."

Eric felt the kids had gone through enough trauma with their father in a wheelchair, his death from cancer, and then Eric's marriage to their mother.

"To be honest," Eric said, "it was horrible for me to move into their house." He said he got rid of almost everything he and his deceased first wife, Debbie, had accumulated in 27 years of marriage.

"I feel as though I went to a hotel with my clothes and toothbrush two years ago and never got to go home again!" Eric is honest in admitting that if he truly realized how difficult the adjustment was going to be, he might not have married again.

How does he cope with the trying times? "I was getting angry a lot and feeling hurt," he said. "I felt like an outsider." But he says counseling has helped him make progress. He claims, as others do, that rejection from stepkids "can cut your heart to the core."

But Eric does not believe in divorce—and he truly loves his wife—so he prays a lot and seeks solutions when things are beyond his control.

So what do kids—especially teenagers—really want and need? For many stepparents it's a guessing game. They want affection one minute and to be left alone the next. They want your attention and time but then abuse you with words and hurtful looks. We all know from experience how challenging it is to anticipate and then meet those needs and wants.

From Angry to Angelic

"My stepdaughter, whom I call my daughter, was my husband's gift to me on our wedding day," said Eva Marie Everson. "She was two years old at the time—so precious. As she grew up, however, this darling child became one of the most angry children I've ever encountered."

Eva Marie said she tried to love her not only as a parent

but also as Christ would want her to. "At age 13 or 14," said Eva Marie, "my husband and I forced her to attend a youth retreat where we were the chaperones."

While recalling the incident, Eva Marie had to laugh. "The story itself is almost comical," she explained. "Before we left, Ashley shouted, 'I'm not going!' On the way there, she relented a bit. 'OK, I'm going—but I'm not getting out of the car.' After we arrived she said, 'OK, I'm out of the car, but I'm not going to participate.' Then while participating, she added, 'I'm participating, but I'm not happy, and there's *nothing* you can do to change that!'

"Well, during that weekend Ashley became a born-again Christian," said Eva Marie. "She has served the Lord faithfully since that time, and we're so proud of her. Today I can say that she is so *in* my heart that it's amazing to me that she was never *under* it!"

SURVIVAL TECHNIQUES

"When we were still newlyweds," said Donna Wyland, "my four stepsons came to spend the summer with us— three long months with four loud stepsons and my six-year-old daughter. The boys played their rock music entirely too loudly and played pool into the wee hours of the morning. We could hear the billiard balls hitting against each other two levels below our bedroom. Needless to say, that led to immense problems. My husband and I did not get along very well that summer, and that's putting it mildly. I went through major mood swings and many hours of anger, and that eventually led to depression.

"But through it all," Donna said, "I knew God was there—even though at times I couldn't feel His presence. I was convinced then, as I am today, that He brought my husband and me together for a reason, and I'm determined to walk the road to the end."

Donna said she spent many hours alone in her bedroom

upstairs or she would take her young daughter to the book-store or coffee shop to get away for a while.

She also took long walks on a path behind their house "to be in nature and to get my thoughts and feelings centered again," she said. "It was never easy, but I'm proud to say we've survived. Hopefully easier times are ahead."

If you're feeling the challenge of being a stepparent to teenage boys and girls, you need all the help you can get.

Following are some of the things I believe our teenage stepchildren really need and want from us. I've distilled what I've learned down to seven points. Certainly there are others, and you can add to the list. I hope you'll feel encouraged.

Comfort. Teenagers need our comfort as they navigate the rough waters between adolescence and adulthood—especial-ly those who go back and forth between two households. They must continually adjust to different house rules, differ-ent personalities, different customs and values. A child of five or six will crawl into your lap and ask, as my grandson does, for a "'nuggle."

Of course, a young person of 15 or 16 is not likely to do that. And if that teen is your stepson or stepdaughter, it's even more unlikely. Nevertheless, he or she needs a "'nuggle" now and then. It can take the form of a warm hug, a smile, a caring word, a listening ear.

Martha Rogers had a stepmother whose affection took many wonderful forms.

"Faye married my father when I was ten years old," she said, "but she didn't become a part of my life until I became a teenager. She brought guidance, security, and stability when I most needed it."

Family laws in 1950 allowed Martha's mother full cus-tody of her and her sister and brother. "Mother didn't want us to be with Dad if Faye was there. My grandmother knew we needed Faye in our lives so she made arrangements for us to visit her house on the weekends, and she invited Dad and Faye to come for Sunday dinner while we were there.

"I'm thankful today that Mammy made the effort, because it resulted in Mother allowing us to spend three weeks with them every summer."

The time Martha spent with Faye and her father were happy and comforting days of travel, camping out, and getting to know her stepmother's family. "She had rules," Martha recalled, "but none were unreasonable."

Compassion. Teens also need compassionate parents— moms and dads who remember what it was like to deal with hormonal changes, emotional swings, academic challenges, and peer pressure. My husband and I found that our teenagers were more cooperative and positive in their outlook when we focused on nurturing rather than demanding.

Charles was an especially good listener, so the kids gravitated toward him when they had problems. I was the fun one, and they came to me when they needed a boost. We would take in a movie or spend an afternoon shopping or sightseeing. I also found that at such times they would open up and talk more about their lives.

Martha's stepmother provided a safe haven for her after she graduated from high school.

"I was then free to live where I chose," said Martha. "Dad and Faye bought a house so I could move in with them. Mother decided that if I was going, they had to take my sister and my brother too."

The five of them became a family. Martha's father and stepmother made it possible for Martha to attend college so she could pursue her dream of becoming a nurse.

As parents, we must take the lead. Instead of getting on their case about school work or making a statement through unreasonable punishment and withdrawal of privileges, sit down and ask your teens to tell you what's going on. What hurts? What doesn't make sense? Why is school a drag? What is it about their teachers or friends or feelings that seems overwhelming?

Can you imagine the relief they would feel if they had a

mom (stepmom) and dad (stepdad) they could turn to with such intimate emotions and experiences, and individuals they could learn from by example?

Connection. Teenagers are often curious about their heritage and that of their stepparents when there's been a divorce and remarriage. They want to know they belong to something permanent—a system that has roots.

Martha said Faye's love for her and her brother and sister became evident when Faye started introducing them as her children rather than stepchildren.

"Then I began introducing her as 'my other mother,'" said Martha. "I was proud she cared enough about us to want to be our mother."

Faye's large family became Martha's family too. "We acquired more aunts and uncles and cousins and spent many happy hours with them," she said. "Mama Sharp became another grandmother for me to love, and my sister and brother and I were always included in Sharp family reunions, even though we weren't blood relatives."

Some parents and stepparents, unlike Martha's, don't want to discuss the past. By making such conversations off-limits, however, we're telling our teens that only part of their lives is valuable—the part that includes the new blended family.

You can do something different. Invite your stepchildren to talk about their other parent and relatives, to bring items into your home such as holiday decorations, books, even photos, so they'll feel connected to both sides of the family. You can certainly create new customs in your blended family, but don't throw out the old.

For example, if your relationship with your stepchildren's natural parents is intact, you might include them in your family celebrations and special dinners. My husband's ex-wife, who is unmarried, comes to our home several times a year for birthday and holiday dinners, and we see her at my stepson's home whenever we visit.

It has been very meaningful to my stepchildren to know

their mother is a welcome part of our lives and that she's loving toward us. My husband has also continued to be helpful and kind to her. She has been deaf since birth, so she can use some extra care, and he's happy to provide it. He helped her move into a new apartment when she came to California from New York, and a few years ago he surprised her by shampooing her carpets and hand-polishing all her furniture while she was out of town.

For a time during their marriage, Darlene and Lew Riggan invited Lew's ex-wife to their home for holiday celebrations. This made it easier for everyone, Darlene agreed. The children could enjoy a day with everyone together in one place instead of traipsing from one home to another.

This is a good illustration of the importance of using wisdom and prudence as you create new traditions or maintain old ones. Not every relationship can bear close contact between all parties. But when possible, it's worth making the effort—for the sake of the children, who are usually the ones who pay the greatest price when parents break up.

Consistency. Being consistently available to our teens is also essential. If we're to make a go of it, we need to teach and observe shared values, house rules, time for fun, honest communication, and accountability. This may require periodic family meetings where you and your teens talk about what's important and then establish a code that everyone is willing to live by. It also includes simple respect for the basic needs and wishes of the other person.

With my stepdaughter, for example, I found the best way to relate to her was from a short distance. I was consistently friendly but not too talkative. Privacy is one of her key values; one of mine is sharing experiences. As I honored hers, she began to honor mine.

Companionship. "I loved cooking," said Martha, "so Faye let me create and serve the meals when I came home from college for the summer or on weekends."

Martha admits she never liked housecleaning, but she

learned quickly how chaotic life can be when chores are ignored. Faye made it look easy! On her days off she took care of the house and sang as she went from room to room. "We worked along with her and learned many of the old hymns and how singing can make work go faster," Martha said.

Faye and Martha's dad believed in befriending other teens as well. They led a Bible study for young people at their church and made sure Martha and her brother and sister attended regularly. "I realized early on that nothing could be done in secret around a church where your parents are well known," Martha added with a smile.

There were cozy times, as well. "I'll never forget the tempting aroma of bacon frying on an open fire in the crisp morning air when we camped out in the Ozarks," said Martha. "The summer between my freshman and sophomore years in college, we traveled to Detroit to visit Faye's sister and her family.

"Despite getting lost in Kentucky, having car trouble in Ohio, and weather too wet for tent camping in Tennessee, Faye always had a joke or story or some other distraction to make things easier to bear."

Continuity. Faye not only was able to give her teenaged stepchildren what they needed but also gave them what they wanted—a sense of continuity. They were not guests in her home; they were her family, and they remained so until she died.

"My stepmother never tried to replace our mother in our lives," said Martha. "She just wanted to be available when we needed her. I loved my mother with all my heart, but my heart had more than enough room and more than enough love for my stepmother too. I only wish I had told her that more often."

For Darlene, the key to continuity is "to be a good other mother, rather than trying to be a better mother than the children's natural mom. They'll always love their mother, no matter what, so it's best to treat her with respect."

Correction. "My stepsons need and want unconditional love and acceptance—no doubt about it," says Donna Wyland. It also appears, however, that they want correction and their parents' opinion—though they may not ask for it. Most teens don't.

"Sometimes it seems they do things just to try to shock us as traditional Christian parents. We've been through tattoos on two of the boys, ear piercing on the same two, which lasted about a year, long hair that took me back to my high school days in the 70s, and one tongue piercing by the oldest son, which was rather short-lived."

She recalled one night when she and her husband took their oldest son to a nice Italian restaurant for dinner. "Before we ordered our food," she said, "my husband turned to his son and told him that he really struggled with his tongue piercing. He asked him how in the world he kept it clean.

"With that, my stepson asked my husband if he wanted him to take it out. As soon as his dad nodded affirmatively and said yes, my stepson immediately unscrewed it and gave it to my husband, who in turn handed it to me!"

Donna said she still has it in her jewelry box to this day. "When my stepson is 40 years old I think it might be fun to pull it out and remind him of his interesting display of independence as a teenager," she said.

Give your teenagers what they need and want—a place in the new family to call their own. Then love them with everything you've got! Soon you'll have a strong one-on-one relationship that will last long after they leave the tumultuous teenage years.

BUILDING A STRONG ONE-ON-ONE RELATIONSHIP

1. Which of the seven points in this chapter do you feel your teenaged stepchildren are most interested in receiving from you?

2. In what way can *you* best meet one of their unspoken needs?

3. What do you need and want to give your stepchildren that will be a lasting contribution to their lives?

8

Being There for Adult Stepchildren—Even When You Don't Feel like It

STEPPARENTING IS ONE OF LIFE'S MOST challenging undertakings. Committing to the long haul, staying the course, speaking the truth, standing up for your values, and being a beacon of light and love through the years takes courage, stamina—nothing short of the grace of God. But when a stepparent is there for a stepchild—even when that stepchild is grown and on his or her own—amazing things can occur for everyone involved.

I have to admit that I'm guilty of not following my own suggestions. There have been times when I was not there for my adult children or stepchildren. They needed me to listen, and I talked instead. They shared an experience, and I gave unwanted advice.

It's only now, in the afterglow of years of counseling and personal experience, that I'm able to see the need for being there even after our stepchildren are grown.

Today, however, when many families are scattered across the miles, stepparents and adult stepchildren may not come together as often as they did years ago, when life was simpler and family members lived closer to one another.

Some stepparents, on the other hand, are indifferent, even cold, toward interaction with their older stepchildren. Perhaps they feel they earned their freedom and they're now going to make the most of it. So they beg off from a get-to-gether, sending a check or gift instead.

But to ignore these opportunities to continue participating in the lives of our stepchildren drains the life out of the family network that sustains us. When we stop being courteous, exchanging sympathy and congratulations, or attending solemn and joyous events alike, we cease to be present to one another, and our relationships die.

However, when we do sustain the caring gestures—the little remembrances, the thank-you notes, sharing food and gifts—we give and receive the love and joy of family life. The best gift of all is our presence. When being there costs us some effort, the effect can be truly moving.

What occasions are most important? Birthdays and holidays head the list. Athletic events, educational programs, and victory celebrations follow closely. But there are less obvious ways to express your caring—like visiting your adult stepchildren when they're ill, taking care of their children, walking through a difficult emotional trial with your stepchild, or attending your stepson's or stepdaughter's office baseball game or employee recognition banquet.

How can you *best* give the gift of yourself to your adult stepchildren? Here are some ideas to consider.

Be Positive

When your stepchildren want you to be part of a celebration, do you immediately think of a reason why you can't be there? You have to work, you're too tired, or you're busy with some activity of your own, or you're just not that interested. If you're such a person, start training yourself now to say yes anyway—instead of thinking up excuses. What better way to show you care than to show up? Ask the Holy Spirit to change your heart and adjust your attitude.

My brother-in-law Harry's operating principle is "Never say no to an opportunity or invitation!" This may not always be practical, but what a great outlook!

The apostle Paul reminds us in Phil. 4:8 what to think on: "Whatever is true, whatever is noble, whatever is right, whatever is pure, whatever is lovely, whatever is admirable— if anything is excellent or praiseworthy—think about such things" so that our attitude will be right before God and before those we love.

In light of this advice, consider your own patterns. Must you say, *No,* or could you just as easily work things out and find ways to accept invitations? Keep in mind that your presence can be a greater gift than anything material you could send in your place.

An invitation often received to anniversary celebrations for couples who have been married many years says it all: "No presents, please. Just your presence."

God calls us to right thinking. We must respond with right action. "Do what is right and good in the Lord's sight, so that it may go well with you" (Deut. 6:18)—and with your stepchildren.

Be Available

Sometimes it's difficult to be at the ready, but when we manage to be there for our stepchildren, to share the ups and downs of their lives despite the inconvenience of travel, expenses, or schedules, we may be astonished at what a difference our presence can make.

A woman I happened to meet once shared with me that her stepfather flew from New York where he was living to Oregon for her graduation from medical school. Her mother had died several years before, but he maintained his relationship with her and stayed interested in the joys and sorrows of her life up to the time of his death.

Being available to your stepchildren, however, doesn't always entail long-distance travel or financial hardships. We all can think of other less complicated times that don't involve expensive flights or long drives. These are times when just showing up could make all the difference, when getting there may require little more than a few steps to visit our nearby adult stepchildren, a couple of hours to attend a function that matters to them, or a few moments with a stepdaughter or stepson who needs a bit of parental comfort.

For example, Martha's stepmother, Faye, stood in for her birth mother at Martha's wedding because Martha's mother couldn't make the long trip from her home. "Faye held my hand when my first son was born and helped me the first week at home," she added.

"Even though she had no children of her own, she knew exactly what to do to teach me about caring for my new baby. She just wanted to be available when I needed her. At a time when divorce wasn't popular and a stepmother was someone to hate, God kindly and lovingly gave me Faye. I thank Him for her fifty years of love and sacrifice that helped mold me into the Christian I am today."

Be Responsible

Sometimes it may be necessary for you to miss a solemn or special event in the life of one of your stepchildren. You may feel sad or embarrassed about it, so you make light of it or don't mention it at all. Gradually you notice a breach in your relationship. Don't let guilt compound your absence. If you didn't go to the ceremony, you can still go to the person. Share your feelings about this with your stepson or stepdaughter. It's amazing how restored you'll both feel once you acknowledge the absence and deal with it.

Be Fun to Be Around

Some stepchildren have to brace themselves for their weekend visit with a stepparent. But Walter feels just the opposite about his stepmother. If there's a party or a picnic, she's right there leading the way.

Not everyone is as energetic and bubbly as this woman, but every stepparent can be fun in his or her own way. What can you contribute to your relationship with your adult stepchildren that will foster your enjoyment of one another?

When they see you coming, do they run *to* you or *from* you? It's up to you to make a difference by being at least pleasant—and better yet, fun—to be around.

Be Respectful

.Many stepparents struggle with this issue. They view their adult stepsons and stepdaughters as kids who need to be reminded, cajoled, advised, managed, or manipulated instead of individuals who deserve respect.

In 1992 Susan Titus married Dick Osborn and became a stepmother to three adult children: Eric, Robyn, and Rick. During Susan and Dick's courtship, Dick's 26-year-old son, Rick, who is retarded, phoned Susan and asked, "When you marry my dad, will you be my mom?"

Susan answered, "Yes," immediately.

"Won't you be my mom now?" he asked. "I don't want to wait until next year!"

These new relationships have blessed and challenged Susan and have taught her a lot about respect. She has emotionally supported Rick through his marriage to Christina, who is also retarded. Susan and Dick have mentored the young couple through the births of their two sons and the overwhelming circumstances that resulted.

"I love being Rick's mom," said Susan. "Even though he is now an adult and is living on his own, I accept phone calls from him on my toll-free number any time of the day or night. I make time to listen to his latest concern or share in his joy. I realize that all his life Rick will be a child mentally, so he will always need me."

Susan said she has not tried to be a mother to Eric and Robyn, who are grown, married, and have children of their own. They also have their birth mother, who is a big part of their lives. But recently during an outing with Robyn and her husband, Susan was so pleased when Robyn introduced her and Dick to her friends as "my parents."

Be True to Yourself

One of the most important gifts you can give your adult stepchildren is your true self—your special gifts, your personality, your unique viewpoint on life. I believe our stepchildren respond to that individuality even more as they grow older. They appreciate the special ways in which we express ourselves in our relationships with them.

My husband, for example, loves music, art, and theater. But he also enjoys hard physical work. My children—his stepchildren—as well as his own son and daughter can call on him to help build a fence, plant a flower bed, or move furniture. And they all enjoy his company at a baseball game, at a play, or over a good meal.

One stepson I spoke with said he and his stepdad have been growing tomatoes together for 30 years. "He knows more about tomatoes than anyone I can think of," said Todd. "As I get older, I notice how much I appreciate this part of our relationship. It's more than his knowledge. It's hard to define. I've always felt safe around my stepdad, and I want to be like that for my stepkids."

Some stepparents go to the other extreme. They're so concerned about the boundaries set by the birth parents that they remain in the background—even after the stepchildren are living on their own.

Our role as stepparents of adult children presents new challenges. But if we're sincere, honest, open in our communication, and respectful of them as individuals with choices and responsibilities of their own, I like to think they'll respond in a positive and supportive way.

For example, Darlene Riggan says she tries to be a good example of Christ's love. "I don't preach to them. They already know that I'm a devoted Christian." But she does share her faith in ways that may spark some interest.

"I have given my stepdaughter and daughters-in-law subscriptions to Christian magazines and invited them to women's luncheons," said Darlene. "And we often talk together of spiritual things."

LOOKING FORWARD

I believe our stepchhildren really do want our presence, our input, our help, and our wisdom. But at the same time they don't want to feel smothered, patronized, or rescued. Perhaps the best way to strike the balance we all wish for is to talk things over. Ask your stepchildren what they want from you, and tell them what you want from them. Be willing to acknowledge that you both may be breaking some new ground and may require an extra measure of patience with yourselves and with each other.

When in doubt about what to do in such situations, listen to the Holy Spirit. Call on Him. What is He guiding you to do? Watch for His presence in areas you may have overlooked.

"The Spirit is what we perceive with rather than what we perceive, the one who opens our eyes to underlying spiritual realities," claims Christian writer Philip Yancey (Philip Yancey, *Reaching for the Invisible God* [Grand Rapids: Zondervan Publishing House, 2000], 148.)

When it comes down to it, there's no excuse good enough for not being willing to open our eyes. No excuse, no matter how well we rationalize it, can make up for these missed opportunities to participate. We have only *this* moment to act upon before it slips away forever.

Your sheer physical presence may be the most you can muster at times, but don't underestimate it.

SAYING YES TO LIFE

To be there with and for our stepchildren involves the willingness to take on their joys and sadness. This is much more than merely doing one's duty. It's an opportunity to connect heart to heart.

"It is only with the heart that we see rightly," said Antoine de Saint-Exupery. "What is essential is invisible to the eye."

Jesus made it clearer still: "The good man brings good things out of the good stored up in his heart" (Luke 6:45).

As we're there for our stepchildren, God is there for us, encouraging us, inspiring us to deeper expressions of love and understanding. Sometimes it takes only an honest, heartfelt word to be truly there for another person.

For some, nothing could be more difficult than waiting on the Holy Spirit to guide them. They want to fix, change, manage, and control—especially when they see pain, sin, or ignorance in their adult stepchildren.

Mary Jane's stepchildren, for example, "continue to struggle with self-esteem and peace in their lives even in their 30s," she says. "I feel they need to see me as a person they can trust, one who is consistent in giving them unconditional love. I need to walk my talk and be here for them." She also admitted she does not always reach her goal. Challenges continue even though her stepchildren are grown and living on their own.

She handles the difficulties by praying with her running partner, who is a great friend and a "fantastic listener," she commented.

When things are tough and she realizes she can't change or fix the problem, Mary Jane stands on a verse in Paul's second letter to Timothy: "God did not give us a spirit of timidity, but a spirit of power, of love and of self-discipline" (1:7).

Sandy, too, leans on the Lord for guidance. Without His presence in her life, she said she would not have achieved the relationships she now enjoys with her adult stepchildren.

"I've been given more by being a stepmother than I ever could have imagined," she said. "My stepchildren are kind, loving adults who are committed to the Lord Jesus Christ and who know they are deeply loved by their stepmom. We've moved beyond acceptance and respect to deep, genuine love for one another. It took a few years, and I give all the credit to the Lord Jesus, who taught me about sacrificial, unconditional love."

BUILDING A STRONG ONE-ON-ONE RELATIONSHIP

1. How can you "be there" for your adult stepchildren in a way you haven't before?

2. In what small way can you begin saying "yes" to life when it comes to your adult stepchildren?

3. Find a scripture that fits your relationship with your adult stepchildren, and pray it daily.

9
When Divorce or Death Occurs

KATHLEEN WEPT OPENLY AS SHE CONFIDED the news she had just received. Her stepson, Rob, and his wife, Carla, were separating. They hoped to work things out, he had told his stepmother, but right now they needed time apart.

That conversation took place five years ago. Rob and Carla did finally work things out, but not as Kathleen had hoped. They divorced three years ago after several attempts to live together again.

Today, her step-grandchildren, Annette and Michael, live with their mother a thousand miles away from Kathleen and her husband, Bill. Carla has since remarried. Rob lives alone and has the children for a month each summer and for a week during Christmas vacation.

"I used to see them every week," Kathleen said after a recent visit. "I miss them terribly. And they're growing up so fast."

Our friend Beth, also a stepmother, joined our conversation as we chatted over tea and a muffin. "I know what you mean," she told Kathleen. "Ever since Lou and Carol and the twins moved, I feel like part of my heart has been ripped out."

Beth meant to be supportive, I'm sure, but the two situations are entirely different. Beth's daughter and son-in-law, Mitch, are still married, and their move was job-related since

Mitch is in the military. Beth sees them twice a year, and she speaks with the children and their parents several times a month.

Unlike Kathleen, Beth does not have to contend with the complications of remarriage, step-grandparents on the "new" side, potential jealousy from the new spouse, or a change in family patterns such as holiday visits, gifts, phone calls, and so on.

Being separated from your stepchildren by geographic distance is not the same thing as being separated from them by death or divorce. If a person has not been through either one, according to those who share this experience, there's no real way of knowing what's involved.

Kathleen, however, knows firsthand. Her stepdaughter-in-law's new husband wanted to limit the stepchildren's contact with her—"because Bill and I remind him of Carla's first marriage to our son, and he doesn't want to deal with that." Carla openly admitted this to Kathleen.

"Our former stepdaughter-in-law could do something to help our situation," she added, "but now that they're so far away, she does almost nothing. We've made various attempts, offering to fly the children here for a summer visit, meeting them halfway somewhere neutral, babysitting while she and her husband go on a vacation, or whatever," said Kathleen. "But nothing's changed. And, of course, we miss Carla too. She was an important member of our family for years."

Kathleen and Bill are not alone. Each year thousands of stepparents become the victims of their adult stepchildren's divorce. If, as statistics indicate, one in two marriages now ends in divorce, that leaves a lot of stepparents on the sidelines.

All three of Darlene Riggan's stepchildren were divorced—one divorced twice. "I believe the Holy Spirit kept me calm and used me to give objective advice, which they all asked for and seemed to accept," said Darlene.

"At their request I was a witness in court for the younger son, counseled with the daughter's husband in an attempt to keep them together, and helped the older son get visitation rights with his children. In all my efforts, the Holy Spirit gave me comfort, patience, and guidance that helped me to help them depend on God.

"I believe the best way to handle these challenges," she added, "is to forget that you're a stepparent and simply love the child as your own. We rarely use the word 'stepmother' or 'stepchild' in our family. During all three children's divorces, they talked with me as much or more than with their birth mom. They know I care, and they seem to value my opinion."

Darlene also stated without hesitation, "I know of no other answer than to turn to God in these and all situations. He has me here for a purpose, and I desire to serve Him."

A shift in the relationship between stepparents and stepchildren and step-grandchildren is inevitable as the adult stepchildren relocate, remarry, and reconstruct their lives in a new (and sometimes faraway) place and take their kids with them.

You may not have anything to say about those decisions, try as you might to change, fix, reason with, and even understand their point of view. The truth is, the outcome is out of your hands, and according to those I spoke with, that's the hardest part to come to terms with.

The *death* of an adult child or stepchild may have similar effects on your relationship with your stepchildren—though the feelings about the event may be quite different. Instead of anger and frustration, as is common with divorce, grief and sadness may be your primary emotions. You also may be anxious and apprehensive as you look toward the future. Your mind may be flooded with questions.

• What if the living spouse decides to remarry and moves away?
• What if the new spouse doesn't like me?

• What if the new spouse discourages my stepchild's relationship with me?

• What if the new spouse doesn't love my stepchild the way he or she deserves?

• What if the death (or divorce) results in the children coming to live with me? Can I handle it? Do I want to?

These are very real questions to which there are no pat answers. Each situation is different and then further complicated depending on the age of the stepchildren involved when death or divorce occurs.

Each person needs to struggle through them on his or her own. Releasing the reins on this area of life, however, will be easier for some than others.

Eileen, for example, said she had to drop all expectations when she heard that her stepdaughter and her husband were divorcing. "For days, all I could do was cry," she said. "I didn't know what would happen next. I prayed that I wouldn't lose touch with my stepdaughter and my darling grandchildren, but it was out of my control. I could write and call and invite them over, but if my stepdaughter said, 'No,' then that was it."

Perhaps *you've* become the victim of an unwanted divorce. You embraced your spouse's children and made them your own when you married their mother or father, and now suddenly they're going off with that same parent, and you wonder if you'll ever see them again.

There's no one way to handle the changes that come about because of divorce, death, and remarriage. Everyone involved gets hurt in some way. And being a stepparent further complicates the situation. Once again, we need to turn to the Holy Spirit for wisdom and guidance.

"But when he, the Spirit of truth, comes, he will guide you into all truth. He will not speak on his own; he will speak only what he hears, and he will tell you what is yet to come" (John 16:13).

SOME POSITIVE RESULTS

One man said he has coped with the change by maintaining "the desire to make it all work for the good of everyone."

Vivian's husband, Don, divorced her, and his children went with him, even though she helped raise them after she and Don were married. But to her they were as much her children as her own, so she and Don agreed that the children could visit her if they wanted to—even if he remarried.

"I did see them fairly often," she said. "They missed me, and I missed them. We had built a bond that could not easily be broken. I know it was the Spirit of God. I never could have made this happen on my own."

RELY ON GOD'S WORD

Whatever the cause of separation—divorce, death, estrangement, or a broken relationship—those I spoke with urged others in a similar situation to turn immediately to the Lord's Word. Although there are many good books on these subjects that offer practical and spiritual help, no comfort, advice, or wisdom compares with the Word of God. Garner those Scriptures that suit your family life, and bring them to mind readily and often. Following are some examples to consider.

Take your worries to the Holy Spirit, not to your stepchildren. "God is our refuge and strength, an ever-present help in trouble" (Ps. 46:1).

Some folks have found it helpful to keep a journal, especially during trying times. Write from your heart. Then listen for the Lord's response. The Holy Spirit will enlighten and strengthen you to take the appropriate action. "It is the privilege of every one of us to be filled with the Holy Spirit's power," wrote Dwight L. Moody. (D. L. Moody, *Prevailing Prayer* [Chicago: Moody Press, 1987], 5).

A life without prayer is a life without power, and the reverse is true as well. A life *with* prayer is a life with power. Let us pray often for our stepchildren.

Focus on your stepchildren, not on their natural parents. "All your sons will be taught by the LORD, and great will be your children's peace" (Isa. 54:13).

During times of crisis, it's the stepchildren who need our time and love and understanding more than anyone. Some blame themselves for the events or feel overwhelmed by the changes they can't control. Instead of wringing your hands or taking on their burden for them, turn to your stepchildren and give them the unconditional love they need.

One stepmother said that all she could do was hold her five-year-old stepson after his daddy moved out. "What can you say to such a young child?" she asked. "I think I was his rock at that point, just as I needed the Holy Spirit to be my rock."

Be a good listener. "Everyone should be quick to listen, slow to speak and slow to become angry" (James 1:19).

Ask the Holy Spirit to help you set aside your grievances and your grief as you listen to your stepchildren. Their perception of the situation and the consequences (especially the consequences to them) will differ from yours. It's important for them to put words to their feelings so they'll not shut down emotionally. Avoid trying to fix or cure or redirect their words. Hold young children as they talk or cry. And with older children and adults, touch them gently, take their hands, or simply look at them while they speak.

Remain steadfast in your support and affection. "The Lord's unfailing love surrounds the man who trusts in him" (Ps. 32:10).

Some stepparents rush in with love and help immediately after a death or divorce—and then lessen their contact over the following months. But we may be the only solid anchor in the lives of our stepchildren for quite some time.

It's important for us to be consistent. That doesn't mean you must contact them every day, give up your own life, or take them in permanently. Stepparents can communicate steadfastness and still live their lives. Phone or visit regularly, if possible, depending on the situation with the natural parent.

The frequency is not as important as the regularity. For example, suppose you take the children one weekend a month or overnight once a week—or whatever you and the other adults agree on. Stick to that, and when you must change the schedule, be up front about it.

Be sure the children know that you're going to be there no matter what, that you can be counted on. Sometimes that knowledge alone can go a long way toward building a secure relationship with you. They may not even take full advantage of what you offer, but just knowing they can if they need to will be healing in itself.

Spend time alone with each stepchild when possible. "He took the children in his arms, put his hands on them and blessed them" (Mark 10:16).

During the transition months following a divorce or the death of a parent, stepchildren—all children, for that matter—need individual comfort and care. This private time will give both of you the opportunity to open up, share, draw close, and express feelings and concerns that might be too personal to disclose in a group setting.

Encourage your stepchildren to share their emotions. "Give, and it will be given to you" (Luke 6:38).

While you're visiting with them, draw out their feelings. It's good to provide fun and laughter and a change of scenery, but some stepparents, hurting so much themselves, fear that if they or their stepchildren talk about the situation, it will have a negative effect. Actually the opposite is true. The more a person can express, the less closed up and weary he or she will feel. You don't have to drag it out of them. Just make it easy for them to talk if they want to.

Express your love consistently. "Dear friends, let us love one another, for love comes from God" (1 John 4:7).

Phone calls, surprise gifts, notes, cards, and the words "I love you" are some of the simple ways you can affirm your stepchildren. Tell them you love them. Remind them that their natural parent loves them. Or in the case of death, take time to talk about that parent and the memories the children have of him or her.

And most important, let them know that God loves them—that He—above all—will be there for them no matter what. Share some meaningful Scripture passages. Encourage older stepchildren to start a prayer journal or to search the Bible for some of the Lord's promises, and then say them out loud each day.

Avoid judging, taking sides, and name-calling. "Wisdom reposes in the heart of the discerning" (Prov. 14:33).

Your stepchildren have only one true mother and father, so don't do or say anything that would damage the relationship between them and their parents. Children are fiercely loyal. They love their parents—no matter what. The Holy Spirit will settle debts and even up scores. We may have strong feelings about how the circumstances came about, but we don't have to share our feelings in a way that will do more harm than good. God is the final judge.

Make your home a safe haven during the stormy times. "The Lord is good, a refuge in times of trouble. He cares for those who trust in him" (Nah. 1:7).

Children of divorce or those who have lost a parent to death often lose their homes. They move away from their familiar neighborhood, attend a different school, and must make new friends. But how wonderful it is if they can count on your home as a safe port—a place to sail into for a good meal, a loving conversation, a happy connection to the tradition and security they once knew!

Find ways, depending on your situation, to bring your stepchildren together in your home. Holiday dinners, birthday parties, summer picnics, and so on at your house can help them build a bridge between the new and old way of life. Of course, a lot of this depends on the cooperation of the surviving birth parent. Naturally, you do the best you can and then release the results to the Holy Spirit.

Be a light on the hill. "I have come into the world as a light, so that no one who believes in me should stay in darkness" (John 12:46).

You may be the only contact with the Spirit of Jesus that your stepchildren have, especially when divorce occurs. Whatever else you may or may not be able to do, ask Him to shine His light through you to your stepchildren. Look for opportunities to speak to them about Jesus, His promises, His Word in the Bible, and His presence in each one of us through His Holy Spirit. Share the forgiveness and love He won for us through His death and resurrection. Bible stories, videos with biblical messages, and stories of your own spiritual journey may provide the light that will lead them into the loving arms of the Lord himself.

BUILDING A STRONG ONE-ON-ONE RELATIONSHIP

1. Go through the Scriptures listed in this chapter and write down ways you can apply their truths to your own life.

2. What do you consider to be your greatest strength in relating to your stepchildren during a difficult time? How might you expand on that?

3. What do you consider to be your greatest challenge in relating to your stepchildren during a difficult time? How might you overcome that challenge with the help of the Holy Spirit?

PART 4
In Step with
the Spirit

10
Spirit-filled Stepparenting

"WHAT DOES THIS *MEAN?*" CATHY ASKED, pointing to a verse in Matthew's gospel as she sat with her dad and me around the dining room table. I had given her a Bible as a gift, and she apparently had been reading it and had some questions. We began talking, and soon we were into a lively discussion about the Sermon on the Mount (Matt. 5:3-10) and how one can actually practice the Beatitudes.

"Blessed are the poor in spirit, for theirs is the kingdom of heaven" (v. 3).

I was no Bible scholar, nor was her dad, but we were so pleased with her inquiry that we moved forward, asking the Holy Spirit to lead us. We didn't have to know the answers to all her questions. We simply needed to be available to listen, to give our perspective, to share our experiences and struggles, and to provide a safe place for her to talk about her own challenges as a young woman.

I remember another time when my stepson, Cliff, called us in a panic while we were away for the weekend. He was a young adult at the time, and he turned to his father and me during a crisis with a girlfriend. His dad listened, counseled him as well as he could, and then read some of the Lord's promises during times of trouble:

"The name of the LORD is a strong tower; the righteous run to it and are safe" (Prov. 18:10)

"Let the beloved of the LORD rest secure in him, for he shields him all day long, and the one the LORD loves rests between his shoulders" (Deut. 33:12).

I spoke with him as well, comforting and encouraging him. We could hear the relief in his voice as he prayed with us and then said good-bye. That day was a turning point in our relationship. I felt we had bridged the gap between civility and intimacy. It brings tears to my eyes just thinking about it.

Stepmothers and stepfathers, perhaps even more than the children's birth parents, have many golden opportunities to nurture stepchildren's natural curiosity about God—regardless of their age or circumstances—and to bring His Word to them.

Self-Righteous, or Righteous in Christ?

"Several weeks ago during my prayer time," said Donna Wyland, "the Holy Spirit showed me that I have been feeling spiritually superior to my husband because my 13-year-old daughter attends a Christian school and loves the Lord with all her heart, while his four sons, age 18 to 26, are about as far from following Christ as they can be."

Donna said the boys accepted Christ as their Savior when they were very young, but now they're on a personal search, reading New Age books and so on.

"When they're in our home we struggle greatly because of their choices in music and television and, at times, their language," she said.

The Holy Spirit helped her see that her daughter is still too young to do much searching on her own. "I can't be sure she'll continue to follow Christ through her teens and early 20s any more than my husband could be assured his children would," said Donna.

Then she realized that sometimes she treated her stepsons as though they were less significant spiritually. "I don't agree with their current religious practices," added Donna, "but I have no right to judge them either. For all I know, they'll be missionaries some day.

"That glimpse of my shortcoming has helped me love them a little better since then," said Donna. "I no longer focus on their current state of lostness, though I pray for them daily. I see now that it's natural for young adults to search, so I'm trying to be more accepting of the season they're in."

SPIRIT-LED PLAY

If your stepchildren are of school age, however, your influence can be profound, because they're still in the formative stage. You can share the Lord in play, in song, story-reading, skits, and conversation. It can be as simple as a few words.

"Jan, I know the Lord. Do you?" four-year-old Susie asked her stepmom as they played paper dolls. Jan said she was taken aback by the child's unassuming statement. Her stepdaughter was visiting for the weekend, and the two were just getting to know one another following Jan's marriage to Susie's father a month or so before.

"I realized in that moment what a great opportunity I had to encourage her in her faith," Jan said. "I told her that I knew the Lord too. Then I waited to see what she said next. I didn't want to launch into a Bible study on the spot! Susie suggested that the paper dolls could be Sunday School teachers. Isn't that the cutest thing?"

Whether you're having a Bible study at home with your family, making cookies together, mowing the lawn, attending a softball game, or playing with paper dolls, there are multiple ways you can share your faith, demonstrating to your stepchildren that your relationship with Jesus is real, practical, and essential to your life.

Discerning what to do and when to do it, however, is what makes the difference between a human stepparent with good intentions and a Spirit-led stepparent who leans on the Holy Spirit for moment-to-moment guidance.

SPIRITUAL SERENDIPITY

When you walk by the Spirit you're likely to be more spontaneous. For example, if you're reading your Bible and a stepchild interrupts you, don't close the book or shoo him or her away. Welcome the child. Pick out a verse just for him or her, and even write it down on a little card he or she can keep. That card may end up as one of the treasures from you that your stepchild will cherish.

You can build on that foundation as the Spirit leads you. You can also play-act certain situations that require a moral action—like returning a toy or found money or choosing friends who share Christian values.

NO TACKED-ON MORALS, PLEASE!

Just as editors don't want writers to tack on a moral at the end of every children's story or build in a sermon-in-disguise, so, too, children do not want their stepparents to tack on a moral or a biblical truth to every conversation they have together. Kids turn away from such obvious stories as well as from obvious adults who turn every visit into a Sunday School lesson.

I'm suggesting that we behave as the Holy Spirit prompts us. That might be a Bible story one time and going on a hike the next. It might include a time of praise at the crack of dawn. Or it might be something as simple and human as comforting a crying baby or listening with understanding and sympathy to a frustrated teenager.

Consider how Jesus related to the people of His time. Sometimes He shared a meal with them, fished, or attended a wedding feast. Other times He cast out demons, healed the sick, raised the dead. Jesus did what His Father in heaven told Him to do. He walked in the Spirit.

FROM THE HEART

You may be squirming at just the thought of approaching the area of spirituality with your stepchildren. And if your stepchildren's natural parents aren't Christians or if they express disinterest or even disapproval, it's all the more challenging.

"When I married my husband, I did my best to be a model of Christ's love to my stepchildren as well as to my own children," said Pat Evans. "I read Bible stories, sang Christian songs, and took them to Sunday School. But I didn't force them to do anything. My stepchildren's mother is Catholic, so most of the time they went to mass with her."

Pat said she must continually remind herself that the children did not choose her as a stepparent. In fact, they had no choice about their parents' divorce. "To me, the most important thing I can do for them is pray, pray, pray, and be an example as Paul reminds us in Titus 2:7-8—"In everything set them an example by doing what is good. In your teaching show integrity, seriousness and soundness of speech that cannot be condemned."

Donna Wyland says the Bible was a great source of comfort to her during her stepparenting years and probably saved her stepchildren from being yelled at more than they were!

"It has given me such peace and hope," she said. "The Book of Job ministered to me at the point of my deepest depression. I felt as if Job were walking through the valley with me. I felt a kinship with him, and I knew without a doubt that the Lord was walking alongside me.

"I've also been a lover of Psalms for many years, and Ps. 139 has given me great hope and peace on many occasions. To think all the days ordained for me were written in the Book of Life before one of them came to be!

"Ps. 138:8 makes my heart sing. It says that the Lord will fulfill His purpose for me. Wow! That verse confirms that I'm exactly where God planned, here with four stepsons and a daughter who challenge and bless me every day of my life.

"The Lord will fulfill His purpose for me, even though I don't understand today exactly what that is. He'll show me daily what I need to know, and I'll cling to His promise to accomplish His will in my life. Isn't that awesome?"

Unlike Pat and Donna, perhaps you're still finding your own way around the Bible and don't feel comfortable or ready to share it with wiggly little kids or laid-back teens who may yawn in your face, or adult stepchildren who don't welcome a stepparent's point of view. Most of us can relate to facing such resistance.

Even if your stepchildren's birth parents are Christians, you may still be apprehensive about inserting yourself into an area of their lives that you feel should be reserved for their mom and dad.

If any of these situations are true for you, I encourage you to ask the Holy Spirit for wisdom about what part to play in the spiritual life of your stepchildren. I believe He does want us to be a light on the hill to them.

In Deut. 4:9 the Spirit invites us to be involved with our children's spirituality without fear: "Only be careful, and watch yourselves closely so that you do not forget the things your eyes have seen or let them slip from your heart as long as you live. Teach them to your children and to their children after them."

This is not about doing spiritual "stuff." It's not about performance. It's about being free in Christ.

"It is for freedom that Christ has set us free. Stand firm, then, and do not let yourselves be burdened again by a yoke of slavery" (Gal. 5:1).

"If you are led by the Spirit, you are not under law" (Gal. 5:18).

LIVING IN THE FRUIT OF THE SPIRIT

In Gal. 5:22-23, Paul writes about the fruit of the Spirit—love, joy, peace, patience, kindness, goodness, faithfulness, gentleness, and self-control. Here are some of the behaviors we can aspire to when we walk in the fruit of the Spirit.

• *Loving* stepparents reflect God's love for us. Caron Loveless reminds herself daily that "the burden is not on our stepchildren to accept us, but on us, as the adults, to accept, include, and enfold them unconditionally with our love."

• *Joyful* stepparents bring a glad heart to every situation— even when things look bleak or even hopeless. They see the Holy Spirit in everything and in everyone. Such people do not look for what needs to be fixed or changed. They look at the blessings that already abound and give thanks for each one.

• *Peaceful* stepparents are those who know that all things work together for good for those who love the Lord. They're not critical or controlling. They don't blow up or sulk if things don't meet their expectations. They don't use words as weapons. Instead, they connect with their stepchildren and their natural parents in ways that lend support. They ask questions. They speak from their own experience. They share a piece of themselves instead of a piece of their mind!

• *Patient* stepparents can handle someone being late for dinner or forgetting to mail their birthday card on time. They share their feelings in a way that keeps their love flowing. They're not compelled to fix or change their stepchildren or their parents. They may ask questions, but they don't unload their raw feelings in the name of love. They trust the Holy Spirit to finish the work He began in each one. And in the meantime, they enjoy their own lives.

• *Kind* stepparents remember that their stepchildren and their stepchildren's parents, like them, are human. They're still learning, growing, and making mistakes. They know instinctively that it doesn't work to discount, diminish, or demean their loved ones with abusive words, gestures, innuendoes, or body language.

• *Good* stepparents don't spoil the present by living in the past. They don't focus on their own lives. They are most interested in hearing about the lives of their stepchildren. They are good people. They are good people to know, good to speak with, good to listen to, good to be with. And they help their stepchildren see and feel the good in all of God's gifts.

• *Faithful* stepparents can be trusted. They say what they mean, and they do what they say. They are true to God, themselves, and the people they're in relationship with. They're sometimes the only anchor in a stepchild's life. And they don't take that lightly. They can be counted on. They'll be there no matter what. They won't bail out—even after divorce or death. They'll not fail to hold up their end of a relationship. Children who have faithful stepparents are blessed indeed.

• *Gentle* stepparents rock an infant to sleep, cuddle a toddler who awakens from a bad dream, and pass out warm hugs to little kids who skin their knees or knock out a baby tooth. They listen to teens and young adults who need an understanding ear. They speak softly, move slowly, and often minister silently.

• *Self-controlled* stepparents keep their own counsel. They increase their praise and eliminate criticism. They take their burdens to the Holy Spirit instead of to their stepchildren or their spouses. They don't withhold their love until their stepchildren shape up, measure up, or live up to their expectations. They know God isn't finished with them yet—or with themselves, for that matter. They weigh what they say before saying it and consider what they wish to do before doing it.

"I'm sorry to say that I haven't always been the best example of the fruit of the Spirit," said Donna Wyland, "but I've always tried to make things right in the end. My daughter told me once that my stepsons really love me because they see me mess up but know I'm always trying to be a better person. I guess that has to be good enough for me for now.

"Hopefully one day God will get me to a point where I love them each so deeply that the fruit of the Spirit will flow naturally from my heart to theirs. That's certainly my prayer."

I have a similar prayer. I'm far from a perfect example of patience and goodness and kindness and love, but my hope is in God, that He will help me live in the Spirit, of the Spirit, and by the grace of the Spirit. I can't do it without Him.

BUILDING A STRONG ONE-ON-ONE RELATIONSHIP

1. Write a prayer praising God for the Holy Spirit and for the guidance the Spirit provides in your life as a stepparent. Be specific about the blessings you've received.

2. What fruit of the Spirit would you like to express more easily and more fully? Why? What specifically can you ask the Holy Spirit to help you do this week to make that change?

3. Go through the fruit of the Spirit listed in this chapter, writing your own definition of each one as it relates to you.

11
Hope and a Future

IN THE BIBLE THE PROPHET JEREMIAH (29:11) reminds us that God's plans for His people are not to harm us but to prosper us, to give us hope and a future. One of the challenges of all parents—step or natural—is learning to relinquish our children to God so that He might bring about His plan for their lives. We can trust Him to guide, guard, and govern them as He sees fit.

"God doesn't really give us our children," says author John White. "He only loans them to us for a season" (John White, "Relinquishment of Adult Children," *Equipping the Saints,* spring 1991, 18). At best we're stewards, caregivers—for a time. Then it's their turn to build their own lives. We hope it will be a bright future and one filled with hope in the Lord—but we can't fully control or predict how their lives will turn out.

The Bible reminds us in the Book of Ecclesiastes that there's a time for every purpose under heaven. If we've done the vital inner work on ourselves that's so necessary to spiritual and emotional health, then relinquishing our stepchildren will be easier than we might expect. We'll no longer feel compelled to use them as a means of working through the unfinished business of our past or as the focus of our desires for the future. We'll take our hands off our stepchildren, releasing them to the victories and defeats that are part of each life. We'll trust God to lead in ways that we could never understand or carry out on our own. And we'll abandon our headstrong attitudes and actions that have so often blocked

127

our stepchildren from the joyful homecoming that can be experienced only after a season as a prodigal.

Just as the Lord wept over our waywardness, we may at times need to weep over our wayward stepsons and step-daughters. We can't save them—only the Holy Spirit can. And wisely and mercifully, He allows them time and space and room to experience and experiment with the gift of life so that when they return they'll be choosing to do so.

That doesn't mean that we abandon our stepchildren or neglect our responsibilities to them as stepparents and as role models. According to John White, relinquishing "means to release those controls that arise from needless fears or from selfish ambitions." (Ibid.)

Ah! Those needless fears—things we fretted about that never came to pass and things that did occur that fear and worry could do nothing to avert or change anyway. And the selfish ambitions—the desire for your stepson to join the family business, for your stepdaughter to be a dancer or a bi-ologist, as you had wanted to be. Or your wish for a child to grace your home with music, so you coerced him or her to study the violin—when *you're* the one who should have tak-en the lessons!

None of this is easy. But as Jesus promised in Mark 10:27, "All things are possible with God." Only with God is it possible to find hope and a future. And only with God is it possible to relinquish not only our stepchildren but an en-tire host of seemingly infallible beliefs associated with them.

Let go of the belief that you possess your stepchildren. Some stepparents view their stepkids as putty in their hands. They attempt to raise children to believe that the parents' needs, feelings, beliefs, and standards are the only ones that matter.

Caron Loveless remembers her stepmother as a perfec-tionist when it came to keeping house but a person who had no idea of how to nurture three young stepdaughters. There-fore, her stepmother controlled their household by her emo-tional absence.

"When we tried to hug her out of desperation and hope, she would ask us what we wanted, or she would shrink back from us," Caron said. She added that she did not remember hearing the words "I love you" until she was 32.

When children are treated as Caron and her sisters were, they emerge from childhood emotionally hungry, sometimes unable to separate their own identity from that of their parents and stepparents.

If you struggle with control issues around your stepchildren—especially if you helped raise them from the time they were very young—ask the Lord to move powerfully in this area of your life. Ask Him to show you the roots of these beliefs and to pull them out so that you and your stepchildren can be freed from the deadly ties that bind you in an unhealthy way. Each one of us comes into this world with nothing, and we leave with nothing, no matter how much we acquire while here.

Our children and stepchildren were given to us. They are likely to remain here for many years after we're gone. Let's give thanks for the time we do have together, relinquish them, and leave the rest to God.

Let go of the belief that your stepchildren are ultimately accountable to you. One of the most challenging beliefs to overcome as a stepparent is the one that our stepchildren are accountable to us—especially if we've had a strong hand in rearing them from the time they were very young, or in the absence of a birth parent.

After we've experienced so many years of looking after them, weeping over their physical and emotional hurts, seeing them through school, participating in their development, and raising them according to what we saw as right and just, it's understandable that we don't easily release the cord of accountability.

You may wish to tell your stepson just one more thing about becoming a father. You may long to take your stepdaughter aside and advise her about the challenge of being a working parent. Or you may feel that whenever your step-children make a decision—from taking piano lessons at age 10 to buying a house at age 30—they should consult with you first.

After all, you have good, sound wisdom about such things, built on a lifetime of trial and error. And you have their best interests at heart. They could learn a thing or two from you—if they would just pay attention! They probably could. But the important thing to remember is that they don't have to.

Mary Jane said she's aware of the importance of her role in the lives of her stepchildren—especially since their natural mother was in constant turmoil while the children were growing up, directing anger at everyone with the children in the middle of it all.

Mary Jane also admits, however, that she fears losing her husband of 24 years over the children. "There's no way the fear should be there," she said. "My husband is a godly man, and we have a happy marriage." But the anger the children show toward Mary Jane, their birth mother, and one another continues to be an obstacle in their family life.

If you can relate to these situations as does Mary Jane, begin praying daily for guidance. Ask the Holy Spirit to give you grace in the trials. It hurts—sometimes deeply—to watch your stepchildren make mistakes with relationships, with money, with school, with their time—with God. It feels good when they seek your advice, your wisdom, your ideas. And it can be humbling when they don't.

They won't always turn to you, no matter how good an example you set. And for some stepparents, their stepchildren will never turn to them. You'll need the grace of God to release them and to see you through those hurtful times.

Let go of the belief that your stepchildren owe you thanks for all you've done. This is another big one. You clothed and fed them, paid for their soccer and swimming lessons. You took them on vacations, sat up nights with them, rushed them to the hospital, and listened to them practice the drums. You helped with homework, volunteered in their classrooms, and threw parties and picnics to honor them. And what did you get for all your love and labor?

"Not much," said one stepmother. "I haven't seen my stepson and his wife for six months, and they live only 30 minutes away."

Another stepmother said she's still waiting for her stepdaughter to talk about the good memories of her childhood. "She has no problem remembering all the things I did wrong," said Rita. "You'd think she'd have a little gratitude."

One would think that. And her stepdaughter probably *will* feel grateful one day. But right now she apparently needs to work through her pain. That's hard on parents and stepparents. I know how it feels. You probably do too.

Eric McNew said he struggles with the lack of appreciation, especially when he's gone over the top to do something special.

"I've learned to lower my expectations to zero. Then if I get anything at all, it's a nice surprise."

There's nothing inherently wrong with wanting our stepchildren to express their thanks. They do have much to be grateful for—just as we do. But there's danger in holding onto a belief that says they have to. You may expect not only words of gratitude but also repayment with their time, their money perhaps, or with a flow of compliments on what a good job you did.

If you fall into that thinking pattern, ask the Holy Spirit to release you from it. Ask Him to fill your heart with peace. Even if you came from an abusive family yourself, you have a lot to be thankful for: You made it. You survived. You still have the gift of life—to now live as you choose. Give your stepchildren permission to do the same. If they someday thank you, relish it and release it.

Let go of the belief that you'll always be a close family. One woman I spoke with said that being closer to her stepchildren is all she wants. "I can't stand us to be cross with one another. I never had any children of my own. Now that their father is gone, they're all I have."

At the time we talked, however, she was distressed over her stepson, who had been estranged from the family for over a year for reasons she wasn't sure of.

I was struck by the fact that she had no room in her thinking pattern for her stepson to be anything but close to her. And she was also quick to abdicate herself of any guilt. Apparently it had not occurred to her that he might be going through a stressful time with his work, with his own family, with his health. Who knows? Whatever the reason, he obviously needed to withdraw for a time.

If your stepchildren want to take some "time off," let them, even if they're still living with you in your home. Support them in their emotional growth, in working out a problem, or in healing some past hurts.

One of my friends released her stepdaughter after a painful episode one day. Months went by with no communication from the girl. She stopped her weekend visits. Then unexpectedly my friend received a card from her for Mother's Day. More time went by with no contact.

Then suddenly the stepdaughter called and invited her stepmother and father to meet her for lunch—her treat with her first paycheck from a part-time job. Their relationship is healing now. Wisely, this woman gave her stepdaughter the gift of time and space when she most needed it.

Let go of the belief that your stepchildren will live by your value system. I remember times in my first marriage when my husband and my father would get into painful conversations about religion. My father was terribly hurt and angry that we had chosen to send our children to public school, especially since we had attended parochial schools ourselves.

Over the years, my father told me how disappointed he was that the traditions he held dear ended with me, since I had not passed them on to my children. Certainly this was not true of every tradition, but that's the way he chose to see it.

During my 30s I stopped going to church. That caused him more pain. I did not set out to hurt him. I did it for myself, because I needed to stop and examine my parents' beliefs, ask some questions of myself, and find my own way. Without that passage I wouldn't be the woman or the Christian I am today. And yet I don't doubt for a minute that my choices then and since caused my father great grief. He admitted it. The gulf between us in that area of our lives continued to separate us until a few years before he died—when I believe he came to understand and respect me as an individual apart from my being his daughter.

Today I observe my son and my stepdaughter sorting out their beliefs, reading, asking questions, assessing their own spiritual direction. At this time, their spiritual direction is different from mine. But I now have my own experience to draw on. I know what it feels like to disappoint a parent. I don't want to put that pressure on my son or stepdaughter.

They have to find their own way in their own time. I know that. I've let go of my belief that they have to live by my system of values—as dear as it is to me.

Let go of the belief that your stepchildren will follow family traditions. I remember as a young wife and mother trying my best to follow the tradition my mother had modeled for the 20-some years I lived at home. She served a beautiful prime rib dinner most Sunday afternoons, complete with whipped potatoes, gravy, fresh vegetables, warm rolls, and dessert. It was a weekly feast we all looked forward to.

But what had worked for her in the Midwest during the 40s and 50s didn't work for me in southern California in the 60s. We were an outdoor family. We liked to ride our bikes, play tennis, and swim. A big meal on Sunday didn't fit our lifestyle or appetites.

It was a great relief to me when one day I suddenly realized that I was not being disloyal to my mother by doing some things differently. I could appreciate her traditions and learn from them, but I didn't have to model every single one.

I'm sure my mother wouldn't have cared one way or the other. That is something I put on myself. But not every parent is that generous. Some feel offended if their children move to another town, leave the family business behind, home school their children, or serve the homeless on Thanksgiving instead of joining the family as generations have done before them.

If you struggle with the belief that your stepchildren should follow your traditions, particularly if you lived in the same household for many years, ask the Holy Spirit to relieve you of that thinking. Pray for grace to relinquish your hold on their behavior. We can't *make* them do anything. Set your stepchildren free—and yourself as well—free to choose what's meaningful to them, to create traditions of their own, and to return to many of those you taught them.

Building a Strong One-on-One Relationship

1. What belief is holding you back from expressing your full love and support of your stepchildren?

2. What step can you take to demonstrate that you've released them to live their own lives?

3. What have your stepchildren taught you about yourself?

12
Love Is All There Is— and It's Enough

PAUL'S TEACHING ON LOVE IN HIS FIRST LETTER to the Corinthians is the best advice I've ever read, and I've applied that advice to my relationship with my stepchildren. When love is the guiding principle, I've needed little else.

This truth came home to me in a fresh way when I read a synopsis of the life of Edward Wilson, who in 1912 went with Robert Scott on his last expedition to the Antarctic as doctor and zoologist. In his diary, Wilson wrote, among other things, about a revelation he had while reading the Gospels.

I found it to be a startling wake-up call for me regarding all of my relationships—certainly the ones I have with my stepchildren.

I began to wonder how one could find out what one was really put here for; and only then it struck me that in the New Testament, and especially in the teaching of Christ, one might be able to write down in one's own words, once and for all, whatever definite directions one could make out from His teaching. . . . It seems to me that across every page may be written as a summary of its teaching, "Love one another in Truth and Purity, *as children,* impulsively and uncalculatingly, not with reasoning and quibbling over what is the best way under the circumstances, but as though I were alone with God in everyone I met . . . faithfully offering them a true love in act and example, and at all costs to myself. Offer them the best, let them take it or leave it, never the second best or half best or best under the circumstances, but the best always." (Devotional E-mail by Peter Kennedy, 2002, "Devotions in the Letters of John").

Imagine offering your stepchildren *the best always* every day no matter what! One way to do it is to love your spouse the best way you can, and to let your children and stepchildren *see* your love for them. The Evanses, for example, displayed their love for one another by setting aside time alone each week. They made Tuesday night their date night.

"When the kids were young and we didn't have much money," said Pat, "we'd go out for coffee. The important thing was that Tuesday night was our time together. It became so important to our relationship that if we missed one, the whole family felt the negative atmosphere it created."

Pat said she and her husband focused the evening on sharing with one another and making important decisions about finances, schooling, and vacations. They also devoted a part of their evening to praying for each of their children individually.

"Even now that we have an empty nest and can talk whenever we want to, we still go out on Tuesday nights," she said.

Pat said the Lord showed her early on in her marriage that love was the most important thing she could give her stepchildren. And He gave her many Bible verses to see her through the challenges. Phil. 4:13 was one she turned to again and again—"I can do everything through him who gives me strength."

He also encouraged Pat by telling her that He would not allow her to experience more than she could handle. "There were times, however," she said, "when I asked Him just how big He thought my shoulders were!"

THE PIVOTAL FORCE

What *is* love? Many persons have at times confused it with pleasing, grieving, manipulating, criticizing, and rescuing. We give our children unwanted advice, pass on our fears, try to control their behavior, instill guilt and pout or shout when things don't go as we want them to. And worst of all, we sometimes do it in the name of love.

"If I didn't love you so much I wouldn't worry like I do."

"I'm doing this because I love you."

"I'm your stepmother. I love you. Can't you just . . ."

"Your stepfather loves you. That's why he . . ."

"If you'll take the advice of someone who loves you . . ."

But love has nothing to do with guilt, worry, fear, and punishment. Paul says, among other things, that love is patient and kind and not jealous, it does not take into account a wrong suffered, and it never fails.

That's a big assignment for any parent to live up to—especially stepparents. But I believe it's important to reach for that standard and to envision what it will be like when we're more able to live by Paul's words.

Love is patient. Stepparents who love with patience don't blow up or sulk if their stepchildren are late for dinner. They don't stop speaking to their stepson or stepdaughter if he or she makes a mistake—even a big one. They share their feelings. They may ask questions, but they don't unload their upset and call it love. And they're not compelled to straighten out their stepchildren with words and gestures that hurt rather than help or with periods of self-imposed silence.

And yet many of us do just the opposite. We're human, after all. Donna Wyland speaks for us all when she says, "As stepparents we need to *choose* to be patient with our stepchildren when things go wrong or when they make a bad decision."

Donna admits that being patient with her own daughter comes so easily and naturally. But with her stepsons it's easier to be impatient and judgmental. "It takes work to love them, because they're the products of two other people—people very different from me. I often disagree with the way their mother parents them, but I need to choose to hold my tongue and to love them the way they are."

Love is kind. On their birthdays and other special occasions, parents who are kind express their love and attention in an individual way. They show their stepchildren that they're among the most important persons in their lives. They've taken the time to get to know them. And because they know them, they care deeply, and they make a point of saying so.

Love does not envy or boast. Loving stepparents encourage their stepchildren to love others as well as themselves—their natural parents, siblings, friends. Such stepparents respect the children's needs, enjoying what time they do have together, and living a full life of their own when they're not together. They don't jealously guard their relationships, afraid that other family members will take their place. They know there's enough love for more than one person.

Love is not easily angered and does not keep a record of wrongs. Stepparents who can express their love with confidence don't spoil the present by living in the past. They don't focus on themselves. And they don't hold their stepchildren hostage over actual or perceived hurts. They go to them and share and listen and ask to work through whatever trial or misunderstanding might have developed. They show by their own lives that they're willing to grow, change, and lean on the Holy Spirit.

Love never fails. Stepparents who realize this truth don't withhold their love until their stepchildren shape up, measure up, or live up to their standards or desires for them. Instead, their stepsons and stepdaughters learn through them that love is faithful, honest, and loyal. Their boundaries are healthy. They continue to discover how they can communicate that truth in a loving and caring way.

When you live by this commitment, what response can

you hope for from your stepchildren? By loving them, you will have helped free them to love God and to love you more authentically. As a result, they'll just naturally become more patient and kind when you're late, make a mistake, or feel out of sorts. And they'll want to spend more time with you because of who you are and what you've demonstrated. They're likely to cheer you on in your own life rather than feel jealous of your victories. They'll know there's plenty of room in your life for them. They'll be less likely to take into account a wrong suffered or to become upset if you misunderstand one another or forget to keep a promise or bring up a past hurt.

They may even model their lives after you and put into practice the same principles they've seen you live out in your life. They'll learn through experience that when stepparents love their stepchildren, they stand by them. They remain loyal to them. They believe in them. And they expect the best from them.

By meditating on Paul's sermon on love and committing to it with action, you'll be teaching your stepchildren that in the end, love is all there is. And it is enough.

Everything else will pass away—hurt feelings, forgotten appointments, misunderstandings, differing viewpoints, friends, beliefs, and practices we disapprove of. But love will not pass away. And love—when fed and nurtured by the Spirit of God—will never fail.

BUILDING A STRONG ONE-ON-ONE RELATIONSHIP

1. How do you express love to your stepchildren?

2. What is the most challenging aspect of loving your stepchildren unconditionally?

3. What part of Paul's passage on love in his letter to the Corinthians speaks most clearly to you?

Words to Consider

Stepparents and Adult Stepchildren Share Their Advice About Building a Strong One-on-One Relationship with Stepchildren

Pat Evans

"Pray. Pray hard. Pray harder. Be the role model. If the kids see you reading your Bible and spending time with the Lord, they will too, eventually."

Favorite scripture: "Bear with each other and forgive whatever grievances you may have against one another. Forgive as the Lord forgave you. And over all these virtues put on love, which binds them all together in perfect unity" (Col. 3:13-14).

Eric McNew

"Be a loving friend; don't try to replace or be the children's father or mother. Affirm and encourage your stepchildren."

Favorite scripture: "This is my prayer: that your love may abound more and more in knowledge and depth of insight, so that you may be able to discern what is best and may be pure and blameless until the day of Christ" (Phil. 1:9-10).

Caron Loveless

"Know well the emotional neediness of your stepchildren. Realize that the burden is not on them to accept you, but on you, as the adult, to accept, include, and enfold them unconditionally. Don't be pushy or impatient for them to come around, but instead, be consistent and believable with your eagerness to become their friend."

Favorite scripture: "When Jesus saw his mother there, and the disciple whom he loved standing nearby, he said to his mother, 'Dear woman, here is your son,' and to the disciple, 'Here is your mother.' From that time on, this disciple took her into his home" (John 19:26-27).

Darlene Riggan

"My advice for stepparents today is to think of yourself as a 'real parent,' because you have the opportunity to express God's love and to be a positive influence on the child. I believe people who marry someone with children need to seriously consider the extra responsibilities they'll have and not go into the marriage if they don't believe they can accept them."

Favorite scripture: "We know that in all things God works for the good of those who love him, who have been called according to his purpose" (Rom. 8:28).

Charles Flowers

"Husbands and wives should be in agreement about discipline and any decisions they need to make before speaking in front of the children. That way everyone sees and hears what's going on instead of relying on what someone else reports. And most important, tell your children and stepchildren every day in some way that you love them—no matter what."

Favorite scripture: "Do not exasperate your children; instead, bring them up in the training and instruction of the Lord" (Eph. 6:4).

Sandy Peckham

"Write down your stepchildren's interests. Then refer to it when you're shopping for a gift or want to surprise them with something they've been longing for. Learn about them, and, of course, pray for them."

Favorite scripture: "[He] is able to do immeasurably more than all we ask or imagine, according to his power that is at work within us" (Eph. 3:20).

Donna Wyland

"Stay in touch with your stepchildren's thoughts and feelings, and be quick to say, 'I love you,' and 'I'm praying for you.'"

Favorite scripture: "The LORD will fulfill his purpose for me" (Ps. 138:8).

Mary Jane

"Pray that God's love will come through to your stepchildren through you and that you can see them through God's eyes. Don't take things too seriously, and practice forgiveness."

Favorite scripture: "Trust in the LORD with all your heart and lean not on your own understanding; in all your ways acknowledge him, and he will make your paths straight" (Prov. 3:5-6).

Eva Marie Everson

"It's all about the children. Put yourself in their place, and imagine yourself feeling what they might be feeling. If you don't try to manipulate but love instead, you'll end up with not only a child but, one day, a friend."

Favorite scripture: "See that you do not look down on one of these little ones. For I tell you that their angels in heaven always see the face of my Father in heaven" (Matt. 18:10).

Susan Titus Osborn

"Your relationship with your spouse needs to take precedence over your relationship with your stepchildren in order for your second marriage to survive."

Favorite scripture: "'I know the plans I have for you,' declares the LORD, 'plans to prosper you and not to harm you, plans to give you hope and a future'" (Jer. 29:11).

Karen O'Connor

"Love. Listen. Encourage. Pray. Be gentle. Be yourself."

Favorite scripture: "May our Lord Jesus Christ himself and God our Father, who loved us and by his grace gave us eternal encouragement and good hope, encourage your hearts and strengthen you in every good deed and word" (2 Thess. 2:16-17).

Are your kids well adjusted? Or do they need an attitude adjustment?

BFZZ083-412-0496

All parents want to raise emotionally healthy children. But how do you make sure your kids are developing the social skills they need to relate to others? Are you leaving it to chance that they'll pick them up along the way? *7 Emotional Skills Every Child Needs* shows you how to nurture vital relationship skills in your children that will help th **In step with your stepchildren building a s** foundation for developing close rela 248.845 O18i   60475 community, and God.